Summer flowers

HANNEKE VAN DIJK

REBO
PRODUCTIONS

© 1997 Zuid Boekprodukties, Lisse, the Netherlands
© Published by Rebo Productions Ltd.
text: Hanneke van Dijk
cover design and layout: Ton Wienbelt, the Netherlands
photo-editing: Marieke Uiterwijk, TextCase, the Netherlands
editing and production: TextCase, the Netherlands
typesetting: Hof&Land Typografie, the Netherlands

ISBN 1 901094 502

Table of Contents

Foreword

As simple as a flower
Hans Andreus

A vase of nasturtiums, a sunflower reaching to the sky, a basket of blue lobelias – all flowers which until a few months ago were still seeds hidden in a colourful packet. Seeds of summer flowers, waiting for the moist earth, the first warmth and a ray of sunlight, because that is all they need to germinate. Strewn in the garden with generous hand or sown carefully in a seed-tray, waiting for the first seedling. Formerly sown by the head gardener with his side-burns and flushed cheeks, who scurried between the greenhouses and the open ground and who knew the Latin names for the flowers so well.

The head gardeners of the past are the nurserymen of today. They no longer grow for that one landowner from the big estate, but for everyone who has a garden. The growers of unusual summer flowers are looking for new and forgotten plants. They show us that summer flowers are beautiful, whether those summer flowers are in borders and pots or in baskets and bouquets. They have opened our eyes to the new use of summer flowers. Owners of gardens which are open to the public show us that summer flowers deserve a place in the garden again. Christopher Lloyd of Great Dixter and many others, bewitch their gardens and their visitors with summer flowers.

To create a garden which is just as beautiful, we can browse in seed catalogues, visit nurseries and gardens and read a lot about gardens. In this book photos and text invite you to create an enchanting garden with summer flowers.
As simple as a flower? Actually it is a miracle, a miracle which astounds us year after year.

Hanneke van Dijk

Salvia farinacea 'Renaissance', an unusual sage that looks somewhat like lavender.

What are summer flowers?

Not all plants that bloom in the summer are summer flowers. Summer flowers love the summer and can't bear our winters. They have found an answer to this: a great many of the summer flowers make masses of seed and overwinter in this way.

Other summer flowers can bear some cold and live through one winter as a plant. Still others can survive the winter, but have to be helped. We have to take these plants out of the garden and put them in the greenhouse or, before the frost comes, take cuttings from the plant and bring them on indoors.

Summer flowers then are not only all the annuals and biennials that we can buy in colourful packets of seed, but they are also the cuttings that we can take in the autumn ourselves and keep through the winter. Of course there are borderline cases and some plants can be considered not only as plants produced from cuttings, but also as tub plants. Quite a number of plants are mistakenly considered as annuals.

Annuals The largest number of summer flowers are found among the annuals. The majority of these plants complete their cycle from seed to seed in a single growing season. They are sown in spring, grow, bloom and make seed before the winter comes and in this way provide themselves with offspring. The plants themselves die off. Their whole endeavour is directed towards ensuring enough offspring and therefore they have to produce many flowers. And that is now just what we so appreciate. Most annuals bloom profusely in order to attract the insects that ensure pollination, whereby fruits and seeds come into being. Very many annuals are, therefore, also excellent bee- and butterfly-attracting flowers.

Nemesia *and* Echium *in a colourful border of summer flowers.*

Above left: many summer flowers attract butterflies. Spider flower, Cleome serulata 'Orchid Festival' *with red admiral,* Vanessa atalanta.

6

Biennials
The biennials sail under this cheerful flag too. Some of the very well-known representatives of these are pansies, forget-me-nots and daisies. Because they bloom early, they fill up the gap between the bulbs and the annuals. But they deserve more appreciation than just as stop-gaps. Sweet William, wallflowers, dame's violet, honesty, foxglove and a handful more of these beautiful, often rather 'old fashioned' plants belong to the biennials.

Plants from cuttings
All these annuals and biennials are sown. A number of plants also considered as summer flowers are, however, produced from cuttings. Not a summer flower, but more summer foliage is the grey *Helichrysum*. A fairly new plant, which immediately captured the market, is *Scaevola*. *Felicia*, *Nemesia* and *Malva* (mallow) are not fussy and can be either sown or cuttings can be struck.

Fleuroselect
Sometimes you can come across plants that have earned a medal from Fleuroselect. Fleuroselect, a European organisation of seed and seed-improvement companies, ensures that new cultivars continue to come onto the market. These new strains are assessed in a large number of experimental gardens. If they receive a good assessment they earn a medal. A prize-winning plant has a good life ahead of it, because Fleuroselect is not only responsible for the assessment and award, but also for the promotion.

Two biennials combined: foxglove and Sweet William.

Low cosmea *fits beautifully into a bed.*

Next page: simple and tasteful: harmonising colours.

Summer flowers past and present

Gardens change through the years and the plants change with them. Or should it be the other way round?

In Renaissance and Baroque times the shape of the garden was more important than the plants in it. The ingenious first levels made from shorn box hedges, were brightened up with small, coloured stones. No flowering plants at all were used. As a reaction to these formal gardens, the green landscape gardens were developed, with artificial lakes and hills and especially many trees. The flowers in these gardens played an unimportant role. Sometimes they provided some colour near the house.

During the flowerbed craze summer flowers in contrasting colours were used.

But then golden times came for colourful summer flowers. A host of plants from faraway countries were introduced into Europe. These plants came from countries with a completely different climate and were mostly not hardy here; they were often annuals. This development took place roughly at the same time as the invention of the hothouse. This couldn't have been better and the head gardeners of large estates set to work diligently. Large quantities of summer flowers were sown and planted, not only in the gardens of large country houses, but also in the gardens of the wealthy middle class.

Above left: a cheerful doll's house garden full of summer flowers

The flowerbed craze

The Victorian age was the time of the 'flowerbed craze'. Gardening books from that period advised particularly the use of many contrasting colours and not beds of a single colour. The red pelargoniums jangled next to the purple verbenas and the yellow calceolarias.

A genuine Victorian flowerbed laid out as a colourful star in Tatton Park.

9

The Victorian beds lie like colourful jam tarts in the grass.

The flowerbed craze reached its zenith in the mosaic beds. The design of a Persian carpet was imitated in plants. For these 'carpet beds', as they were fittingly called, many foliage plants such as *Coleus, Irisine* and *Sempervivum* were used. In the colours of a Persian carpet – green, silver, brown and yellow – true masterpieces were created.

The flowering plants used for the beds could not of course be too tall or too rampant. These sorts were banished to the kitchen garden or were allowed to grow in the cottage garden.

Cottage gardens   Eventually the flowerbeds began to pall and a revolution broke out against this stiff and formal manner of gardening. People who did not have a gardener, labourers who had hardly enough food to eat, could not of course allow themselves the luxury of beds full of expensive plants. And yet, they gardened with enthusiasm, be it from a totally different aspect. In any case, the garden had to produce something. For that reason vegetables and herbs were grown in the first place. But flowers also put in an appearance.

The nice thing about summer flowers was that they were easy to sow. And you didn't have to buy the seed; you got it from your neighbour. The same applied for cuttings. And in this way, born from necessity and lack of money, a constant exchange of seeds, plants and cuttings took place.

Next page: Cosmeas and antirrhinums alongside vegetables in the cottage garden.

Gertrude Jekyll, the well-known garden designer of that time, who reacted violently to those monstrous flowerbeds, was inspired by these romantic cottage gardens. She loved to use summer flowers in her famous borders.

Summer flowers of today

What is the situation regarding summer flowers today? We still see poor copies of the Victorian beds, where red salvias, orange African marigolds and blue lobelias blare at you. We still see cottage gardens (allotments) where the neighbour, who is on early retirement, grows the most beautiful vegetables and summer flowers. We see him cycling past with a bag of beans hanging from his handlebars and a bunch of asters tied on his carrier. He doesn't worry about certain trends that dictate the species of aster that you should be growing or which flower is really out of date.

In a cottage garden the plants are even allowed to seed themselves through the steps.

The people who really worry about those things are the modern Victorians, the members of garden clubs, who look for that one plant they haven't got yet. Just as in those days they derive enormous pleasure from their gardens, as do others who visit their gardens. A wind of change is blowing through the gardens, a breeze of new summer flowers. Summer flowers cleverly incorporated into borders, pots and potagers. Summer flowers with subtle colours. Back again, or brought on to the market as new cultivars.

A garden full of summer flowers.

Summer flowers in and round a pot.

The modern Victorians can enjoy to their heart's content as they leaf through the catalogues of the various seed and plant growers. These growers, obsessed by summer flowers, ensure with great enthusiasm that summer flowers again get a place in modern gardens which they so deserve.

Summer flowers every-where

Summer flowers are so unbelievably versatile that they can be used in many more ways than you would at first think. Once you become besotted with summer flowers, there is often no more holding back.

Borders full of flowers

Summer flowers are excellent to use in combination with perennials in a border. Usually the taller ones are used for this purpose.

Spider flowers *(Cleome)* and *Cosmos* are very suitable here; furthermore they combine well together because they come in harmonious shades of white, pink and mauve. Tobacco *(Nicotiana)* combines well in all its species and cultivars, from the imposing *Nicotiana sylvestris* to the graceful *Nicotiana langsdorfii* and the green/yellow 'Lime Green'.

Not only the blue love-in-a-mist *(Nigella),* but also the white, pink and lilac cultivars look beautiful next to the grey foliage of *Artemisia* and pink or blue-flowering garden geraniums *(Geranium)*. Papavers, from common poppies to opium poppies seed freely and the seedboxes of the opium poppies in particular, are an unusual extra. Sunflowers, with flowers a little smaller than the well-known giant variety, also combine well, especially the somewhat paler shades, such as *Helianthus annuus* 'Lemon Queen'. *Ambrosinia mexicana* 'Green Magic', a lesser-known plant with long green plumes, not only brings rest to a border, but also has an unusual scent. And then there is of course dill *(Anethum graveolens),* which graced the kitchen gardens for years until people discovered that the greenish-yellow umbel gives a marvellous effect in the border. The white bishop's flower *(Ammi majus)* – no relation, but it looks very much like dill – is ideal for blending into borders.

A border made up entirely of summer flowers. Above left: newly-planted Nicotiana x sanderae *'Havana Apple blossom' in the course of the summer they will form a gorgeous pinkish-white ball.*

Papaver commutatum *'Ladybird' goes well with* Asperula orientalis.

It is also very suitable as a cut flower. Summer flowers can not only be used to fill up or weave into a border, they can also make up a border without the use of perennials. You can compose this type of border by colour, but by mixing all colours you can also make a variegated whole. Borders composed exclusively of summer flowers usually only reach their peak in August and September, because most plants need 'take-off' time before coming into full bloom.

Within the borders

For a while it looked as though the beds of yesteryear had disappeared, but they are returning in a modern version. Surrounded by closely-clipped box hedging with a standard rose in the centre, they are acceptable again. In formal gardens many summer flowers are still being used to fill up the geometrical beds.

Colour is of course the first thing that strikes you in gardens of this kind and it makes a great difference whether a bed is filled with bold orange African marigolds *(Tagetes)* or with unpretentious blue viper's bugloss *(Echium).* In our own gardens we can also play with the colours of summer flowers and once and for all, have done with the cheap, glaring image they have acquired in the course of the years. Even the most critical gardening club member will have nothing to complain about a box edging filled up by low *Nicotiana x sanderae* 'Havana Apple blossom'.

Ornamental tobacco, Nicotiana, *kept with in limits by a neat box hedge.*

Box shapes filled with African marigolds.

A bouquet of summer flowers from a cutting garden.

Instead of a box hedge, a bed can be enclosed by an edging of 'summer foliage', such as the grey *Senecio cineraria* 'Silverdust' or by a flowering edging plant like pink, lilac or white alyssum *(Lobularia)*.

Good to pick   Many summer flowers are excellent flowers for picking. It is also ideal to arrange a corner in the garden or vegetable patch as a cutting garden. Fortunately, the seed trade has cleverly anticipated this and in their packet-seed ranges they have included a mixture for cutting.

These seed mixtures are becoming well-known and many a garden-lover has sown one of the 'garden bouquets' selected on colour. In every blue, yellow and green, lilac-pink and white mixture sufficient for 6 square metres, there are some 20 different species, well-suited to each other.

There is also a garden bouquet for butterflies, with plants which butterflies love. This mixture has been compiled in cooperation with the Butterfly Foundation, and the flowers bloom from July until far into the autumn. If we sow this mixture of colourful summer flowers we get the butterflies along with it free!

Beautiful cut flowers deserving a place in the kitchen garden or special cutting garden are white bishop's flowers *(Ammi majus)*, the higher cultivated species of snapdragons *(Antirrhinum)*, *Bupleurum*, marigolds *(Calendula)*, larkspur *(delphinium, Consolida)*, sun-

Marigolds are ideal for picking.

16

flowers *(Helianthus)*, rudbeckias *(Rudbeckia hirta)* and zinnias *(Zinnia)*.

The fact that flowers for picking do not always need to have very long stems is proved by nasturtiums *(Tropaeolum)*, pansies and Californian poppies *(Eschscholtzia)*.

The everlasting ones

The bells of Ireland, Molucella laevis, *are well suited for drying.*

Dried or everlasting flowers are unusual cut flowers. The name immortelle is even more beautiful. Picked at the right moment and dried in the correct way, these flowers still give pleasure even in the winter. A summer flower which is specially grown for drying is *Helichrysum bracteatum,* the rustling papery flowers of which are already immortal when the buds open. Or think about *Helipterum Humboldtianum* with grey leaves and yellow flowers.

Helipterum manglesii, formerly known as *Rhodanthe,* has very modest pink or white flowers and mixes well with other summer flowers. The white winged everlasting with the golden centre *(Ammobium alatum)* is also a real dried flower, as are various sorts of sea lavender *(Limonium)*.

Some summer flowers are not real dried flowers but can be dried. The seed-boxes of the opium poppy *(Papaver somniferum)* and love-in-a-mist *(Nigella damascena)*, the bells of the bells of Ireland *(Molucella)* and the plumes of *Ambrosinia* (ragweed) are splendid when dried and are very good to use in bouquets. Many annual grasses, such as quaking grass *(Brizia)* and hare's tail *(Lagarus)*, are also excellent for drying. Drying entails no more than hanging small bunches upside down in a dark and airy place. As soon as they feel crackly, they are dry.

Going up   The climbing summer plants perform tremendously by not only blooming, but also rising to great heights, all in one season. One of the most well-known annual climbers is of course the sweet pea. *Lathyrus odoratus* is the most frequently grown. There are many cultivars of this in the shops.

There is even a shorter version, 'Bijou', that can be used in pots and in the border, without support. The nasturtium also has climbing and non-climbing varieties. *Tropaeolum majus* 'Gleam Hybrids' is a real climber, just like the canary creeper *(Tropaeolum peregrinum)*. Unusual perennials, but not hardy climbers are *Eccremocarpus* (glory vine), black-eyed Susan *(Thunbergia alata)*, cup & saucer vine *(Cobaea scandens)*, morning glory *(Ipomoea tricolor)* and *Mina lobata*.

In pot and   People suddenly discovered that you could do far more with plants
container   than just putting them into a container on the windowsill. Many plants thrive in pots, summer flowers certainly do. The choice in summer flowers is so large that this trend will continue for a while, cer-

Morning glory, Ipomoea, *is climbing in the greenhouse here, but also grows well outside in a sheltered spot.*

tainly now that there are automatic irrigation systems available, so that you can go away for a weekend now and then.

Summer flowers thrive in all sorts of pots and containers. It is important that there are holes in the bottom of the pot or container. But to guarantee that the water runs away, the pot has to be just raised from the ground.

A very stylish solution for this is the terracotta lion's paws. A somewhat simpler solution consists of putting pieces of wood under the pot. The ready-to-use potting compost is suitable as filling. Ensure that there is a layer of pieces of broken pot, gravel or hydroculture granules covered by a piece of anti-rooting mat or fine wire-netting. This prevents the roots from growing through on the way to the holes and clogging them.

Do not fill the pot to the brim: there must be enough room left for watering. Once the plants are in the pots, they have enough nutrients in the potting compost for the first six weeks. After that they need feeding.

Water in the pot Water is just as vital as food. As far as this is concerned, summer flowers in pots need far more attention than plants in the garden. The water in a pot evaporates quickly and even in rainy periods the plants must be watered very regularly, because at that time the risk that the earth in the pots will dry out is greatest – whoever goes around water-

Nasturtiums and petunias hang convivially side by side.

Next page: summer flowers in pots and baskets on chairs and benches.

19

ing plants in pots when it is raining? The rain water, however, particularly if a pot is full with a dense mass of flowers and leaves, runs over the leaves and beside the pot instead of into it. The plant looks wet, but the roots have not had a drop of water. Water plants in pots every day, particularly if the weather is hot, and even twice a day in exceptionally hot weather.

For anyone for whom this is too labour-intensive, technology is at hand. There are various systems which operate on the same principle. An irrigation system of this kind can be drip-watering or a sprinkler system. They can be bought as a D.I.Y. kit and can be built up as required.

Plants in pots   Although very many plants are suitable for pots, one sort will always do better than another. A 2-metre high sunflower will be a bit wobbly in a pot and soon become top-heavy. *Polygonum orientalis* which reaches 1.5 m will also not feel completely at home in a pot. Its smaller brother *Polygonum capitatum,* which is actually a creeper, is very suitable for a pot and even for a hanging basket.

Many ground-covering summer flowers, which are not tall plants, such as *Sanvitalia procumbens,* dwarf nasturtiums *(Tropaeolum), Nierembergia, Nemophila,* lobelia, *Brachyscome, Erigeron karvinskianus* and *Convolvulus sabaticus,* are also particularly suitable. The well-known petunias are still best-sellers for growing in pots and

A beautiful Nicotiana x sanderae 'Lime Green' *in a pot.*

Hanging baskets filled with nasturtiums.

are also acceptable for the critical gardener. It is not without reason that the *Scaevola*, derived from cuttings, has shot up in popularity like a comet. It is a rewarding and long-flowering plant.

Hanging baskets

Hanging baskets filled with surfinias, the new petunia from Japan produced from cuttings.

Hanging baskets remain popular too. You can even buy them ready made up and planted. You only need to give them water and fertilizer. But that is often exactly the problem with hanging baskets. Because there are so many plants in a small amount of soil, the baskets need a great deal of food and water. The watering is really of crucial importance. If you do not have the time or patience for this, do not attempt it, unless you have an irrigation system. If the hanging baskets are well looked after, the result is a breath-taking waterfall of colourful flowers. In Japan a new group of hanging petunias has been developed, the surfinias, which are particularly suitable for this purpose. Their shoots can sometimes be 50 cm long and they bloom profusely.

Sowing or buying

The nice thing about summer flowers is that you can sow almost all of them yourself. Depending on the species you can sow them inside or outside or take cuttings.

Sowing and taking cuttings from plants is not difficult; it only requires some space and thought. For anyone who does not fancy that, there are always the garden centres and nurseries. In general, you will find colourful plants here in all current species. There are a few nurseries which grow unusual annuals – which is a comfort to those who really do not have green fingers or have no time.

Sowing the seeds yourself

The real work begins when the order arrives or the packets of seeds have been bought. On the back of the colourful packet, on which the photo promises miracles, there are mostly very brief instructions regarding sowing. Sowing indoors, sowing directly where the plants are to flower, in a warm place or outside on a seedbed, but how to do it and why is not mentioned.

A strong annual, like love-in-a-mist *(Nigella)*, can be sown directly outside where it is to flower. This is possible from the middle of April. In general, sandy ground is more suitable than clay for sowing seeds. Sandy ground warms up more quickly in spring, while clay remains wet and cold for a long time.

Beginners, in particular, should sow in rows, because weeds can then be seen and removed more easily.

Sowing outside

Plants which really cannot bear the cold, such as zinnias, can be sown directly outside if this is not done too early.

A garden-lover's garden. Everything has been self-grown!

Above left: Californian poppies, Eschscholtzia californica, *which can be sown in September, bloom early the following year.*

Opposite page: Convolvulus sabaticus *is a real plant for propagating by cuttings.*

25

Cosmos, papaver and woodruff. The first one and the last can be sown indoors, the middle one must be sown where it will bloom.

Depending on the weather, they can be sown from the beginning to the middle of May. Sowing directly outside saves a lot of work. The only disadvantage of this is that they bloom a little later, but otherwise do very well.

For certain flowers which have a long growing season, this method is not suitable. Really strong summer flowers like papavers, marigolds *(Calendula)*, cornflowers *(Centaurea)*, larkspur *(Consolida)*, love-in-a-mist *(Nigella)* and Californian poppies *(Eschscholtzia)*, can even be sown in September. This is a bit like the cultivation of biennials.

Sowing biennials

These summer flowers take two years to bloom and are sown in June. They need some time to form a rosette, with which they can overwinter. They bloom the following summer. The nice thing about biennials is that it sometimes seems as if they are perennials because, once sown, they keep on coming back. Teasels *(Dipsacus)*, mullein *(Verbascum)*, honesty *(Lunaria)* and foxglove *(Digitalis)* seed themselves exuberantly, at least in gardens which are not weeded fanatically.

The ground in which the sowing is done must be light and fine. If you sow between other plants, loosen the soil with a hoe. This can be a problem in clayey soil because, of course, seeds do not like lumps of clay.

Next page: antirrhinums, cosmos and evening primrose. All plants you can sow yourself.

26

In this case, a great deal of attention must be paid to breaking the soil down. If necessary, add some sand or peat. Sow thinly and put a marker with the name of the plant where you have sown. This is important: most people underestimate the germination power and cannot imagine that a plant will come out of almost every seed. Fine, small seeds can be mixed with sand, which will enable you to sow more easily.

When the plants come up you must thin them out.

Sowing indoors

The only plants which can only be sown where they are to flower, are plants with a tap root, such as dill and papaver. Almost all other summer flowers can be started off indoors, particularly when the weather is not on your side.

Plants such as petunias and diascias, which have a long growing season, must be sown indoors. This can be done in pots or seed-trays, which are then put on the windowsill or in a frame or greenhouse. Everyone has their own preference in this. The advantage of a greenhouse or frame is, of course, that the plants get more light and do not become straggly.

The light problem can be partially overcome by not sowing too early. Plants which have been brought on indoors may only be put outdoors after the middle of May, because until then there is still some danger of night frost.

A summer border, only a few months ago it was no more than a few colourful packets of seed.

Diascias have more time to flower if they are started off indoors.

Potting compost and seed-trays

The pots and trays which are used for sowing must be clean and the earth must be sterile (so not from the garden). Never use rain water for watering!

These measures should prevent the dreaded damping off. This disease is caused by fungi which attack the roots, causing the seedling to topple over. There is no way of saving them. As a precaution you can hold a few seeds back. Should anything go wrong, you can then sow again.

Do not use ordinary potting compost for sowing, but use special sowing compost. You can make this yourself by mixing two parts of potting compost to one part of peat and one part of sand. Cocopeat, a mixture consisting of coconut fibres, is also suitable for sowing. After sowing, firm the ground gently so that the seeds make good contact with the ground. Cover the surface with a thin layer of sand, using as rule of thumb 'sow as deeply as the thickness of the seed'. Then gently spray the entire surface with a plant-spray – not with a watering can or the seeds will be washed away – and place the seed-trays and pots in a light, warm place, in a greenhouse, a heated frame, indoor greenhouse or on a windowsill.

For those of us who do not have a greenhouse, a heated mat is a solution. The seeds then get warmth from underneath by placing the mat under the seed-tray. The tray or pots are then covered with a sheet of glass or a newspaper. As soon as the seeds germinate, this must be

These nemesias are sown, but some species can also be propagated by cuttings.

Next page: petunias must be sown indoors because they have a long growth cycle.

31

removed. An indoor greenhouse has a special roof by which a warm and moist atmosphere can be created. As soon as the plants have come up and are growing well, it is better to leave the roof off, otherwise the plants could have problems with fungi.

These nemesia and verbena can be both propagated from cuttings and sown.

Taking a bit of distance   As soon as the young plants are big enough, you must prick them out and move them further away from each other in a box, a tray or in pots, using ordinary potting compost. Lift the tiny plants out of the ground with a small stick. During pricking out, the incredible number of seeds in one packet becomes obvious. You usually have far too many plants. Save the rest in case something goes wrong with the plants you have pricked out. After pricking out, the young plants grow well and it is time to put them in a cooler place.

Getting used to the cold   Hardening off, getting used to the cold, has to be handled carefully. If the plants are suddenly brought out of the warm atmosphere into the cold, growth stagnation occurs. Many plants cannot stand 'stress' such as this. They have to acclimatise gradually to lower temperatures. If the thinned-out plants were first on the windowsill in the living room. they can be moved to a windowsill in a colder bedroom, where, in addition, a window is often open. When the weather is reasonable, the plants can be outside, at first only during the day, but later when they are used to this, also at night. An ideal way of harden-

Shrub marguerites, Argyranthemum, are propagated by cuttings.

33

Sutera cordata (Bacopa) *is a real propagated plant.*

ing-off is in a cold frame outside. The cold frame does not have to be a professional frame, but can be a D.I.Y.-job made from wood, stones and plastic or an old window pane. Hardening-off in a frame is easy: first you leave the plastic or glass lying on top, later you let some air in; after that the glass can be left off during the day, and later also at night.

Not sowing, but taking cuttings

Penstemon *(beard tongue) can be sown or propagated by cuttings.*

Certain summer flowers and foliage can easily be propagated through cuttings, like the shrub marguerite *(Argyranthemum)*, *Brachyscome*, *Convolvulus sabaticus*, *Felicia amelloides*, *Lobelia richardii*, *Lantana*, *Heliotropium*, *Osteospermum*, *Sutera*, certain species of *Salvia*, *Scaevola*, *Penstemom* and certain species of *Nemesia* and *Verbena*. The foliage plants which are grown as annuals and propagated by cuttings, are *Helichrysum*, *Plectranthus* and *Senecio*.

Some of these plants can also overwinter frost-free when fully grown, but that is usually more difficult than taking cuttings before the winter and keeping them. The best time to take cuttings is from the end of June to September. The plants are then still healthy and the cuttings have some time to root before the winter sets in. The cuttings must be 5 – 10 cm long and the lower leaves must be removed. Cut them straight across with a sharp knife just under the node, where the leaves are attached. To encourage rooting, you can dip them in rooting powder. Then push the cuttings into a pot with ordinary potting

In the spring you can buy summer flowers galore.

compost, into which you have already made a little hole with a stick. Firm the ground well around the cutting. By putting the pot into a plastic bag, blowing this full of air and tying it off, the humidity around the cuttings remains high and the plants usually root well within a couple of weeks. If necessary, you can pinch the top off, remove any side-shoots and transfer the cuttings into a larger pot.

Buying summer flowers

If you don't like to sow or take cuttings of summer flowers, or you haven't got the time or courage to do it, you will have to buy them as young plants. In order not to succumb to the colour euphoria of summer flowers which meets you at the garden centre, it is advisable to consider first, in your own home, which summer flowers you actually want. Are they going to be planted in a bed in the garden or between the perennials in a border or are you only looking for some plants for the pots on the terrace?

All the summer flowers in this border have been sown.

Browse through the books and catalogues first and make a choice in principle, regarding the kind of summer flowers and the colour. This will prevent you from coming home after a visit to the garden centre, only to find that the plants do not appear to go well together. Take the trouble of looking for unusual varieties, because there are nurseries that grow a large assortment of special summer flowers. Some of them will even sow the desired plants to order.

Next page: the self-sown harvest of a summer: annuals in pots, containers and pumpkins.

Summer flowers from A - Z

In this chapter you will find the most important summer flowers listed in alphabetical order. With the aid of the information given for each plant, you can make a planned choice for your garden.

Achillea   *Achillea millefolium* 'Summer pastels'. A good start, because yarrow is not an annual. However, these summery flowers in pastel shades are easy to sow. If they are sown early, they will flower the first year. The soft apricot, salmon-pink, red, yellow, lilac and orange coloured, 60 cm high flowers are excellent cut flowers. Plant them in a separate corner for cut flowers or mix them skillfully in a border. Their pastel colours are breathtaking.

Adonis   *Adonis aestivalis*, pheasant's eye or adonis, looks rather like an anemone. The bright red flowers with their dark centres contrast nicely with the delicate leaves. They are not demanding and, sown in a sunny spot in the garden, they will flower after eight weeks. The 40 cm tall plants have a tap root and do not transplant easily. This cheerful little red flower used to grow wild in corn fields, but disappeared in 1935.

Ageratum   The *Ageratum houstonianum* displays a great difference between the dwarf varieties and the giants. Short, stocky plants such as the 'Blue Blanket', 'Summit', 'Blue Lagoon' and the white 'White Raven' are suitable for edging and pots. These flat dwarfs have a rather chubbier little brother: 'Blue Ribbon'. If you don't know this, you can wait in vain for them to develop stems, so that they can be picked. For picking and blending in the border, the taller 'Dondoschnittperle' and

Achillea millefolium 'Summer Pastels' is really a perennial. However, it flowers from the first year and must be re-sown regularly, which is why we have included it.

Above left: taller ageratum *is beautiful in the border and as a cut flower.*

'Blue Horizon' are more suitable. 'Bavaria', also sold as 'Southern Cross' and 'Capri', is an unusual bicoloured, blue-white ageratum. 'Old Grey' is greyish-blue. There are also pink varieties.

Agrostemma

The corn cockle, *Agrostemma githago,* is still listed in the flora, but that is unfortunately the only spot where this beautiful corn cockle can be found. The plant is quite rare and is almost only found in the South. All the more reason to grant it a spot in the border. With its pretty mauve-pink flowers, the 60-80 cm tall corn cockle fits in beautifully with other annuals and perennials. It can be grown in a pot and also does very well in a bouquet. 'Milas' is darker, 'Purple Queen' has large purple-red flowers.

Alcea

The difference between annual and biennial hollyhocks is not always clear. The experts even advise sowing all hollyhocks in the spring as annuals, to prevent the plants suffering from rust. The true enthusiast prefers single hollyhocks, which are usually sold as a mixture in a packet of seeds. 'Nigra', a purple-black hollyhock, is an exception to this. But among the double hollyhocks, such as the mixture 'Chater's Doubles', there are some extremely beautiful ones. A beautiful apricot-coloured example is 'Chatteris Double Apricot'. Two rather wilder, but beautiful varieties are *Alcea filifolia* and *Alcea rugosa,* both with single yellow flowers.

*Actually, the single
hollyhock, Alcea,
is really the most
beautiful.*

*Next page: This is how
the pheasant's eye,
Adonis oestiralis,
used to grow in the
wild in cornfields.*

39

Amaranthus As far back as the 17th century, these 'love-lies-bleeding', as they are so romantically named, were being grown. Until the last century, everyone loved them in flowerbeds. After that, this plant was much maligned; nowadays it is again accepted in the garden. There are hanging and erect, green and red plumes. *Amaranthus hypochondriacus* comes with red plumes ('Pigmy Torch') and erect plumes ('Green Thumb') 30-40 cm tall.

Amaranthus caudatus needs a whole metre to let its plumes hang. The species is red; the cultivar 'Viridis' is green. Also growing to a height of one metre, with erect, brown-red flower plumes is *Amaranthus Hybridus* subspecies *paniculatus* 'Oeschberg', which looks lovely in a border. If the plants become too big, you can prune them like a shrub and they will make shoots again.

Ambrosinia Do not expect striking flowers, but fragrant, slender green plumes. *Ambrosinia mexicana* 'Green Magic' is the largest; a 1 metre tall haven of rest in a colourful border. 'Jerusalem Oak' is 50 cm and has a characteristic scent, which not everyone appreciates. The seed can also be bought as *Chenopodium*. It is a nice cut flower for summer bouquets.

Ammi A short time ago nobody had ever heard of it, but now you can already buy it in the florist's.

Green love-lies-bleeding Amaranthus caudatus *'Viridus', used as a dried flower and in the border.*

Left: the beautiful green spikes of Ambrosinia mexicana *'green Magic' lend peace to borders and bouquets.*

The bishop's flower is irresistible and combines well, both in bouquets and in the garden. In the garden *Ammi majus* flowers profusely with lacy umbels which find their way in between the other flowers. *Ammi visnaga* makes somewhat more foliage and 'Green Mist' is greenish-white. The flowers resemble dill; that is why this plant is also known as white dill.

Ammobium There is obviously not much improvement to be made to the winged everlasting, because few cultivars are known: *Ammobium alatum* 'Grandiflorum' and 'Bikini'. The species grows on the sand in Australia and the flowers rustle like paper. The plant feels at home everywhere, as long as it is sunny, in a special place in the vegetable garden or mixed with perennials in a border.
The winged stalks carry small composite flowers, with a yellow heart that develops into a plump little cushion and the rustling white petals fold back.

Anagallis This blue pimpernel has larger flowers than the scarlet pimpernel, *Anagallis arvensis*, that grows wild in the vegetable garden. The scarlet pimpernel can also suddenly have one or two blue flowers. *Anagallis monelli*, subsp. *linifolia* has bigger clear blue flowers and is often mistaken for a gentian.
'Gentian Blue' is a beautiful blue cultivar 20 cm high. Since pimpernel

Anagallis linifolia *only opens its blue flowers in fine weather.*

A lady's mantle, Alchemilla mollis, *of white lace*, Ammi majus. *What a combination!*

flowers only open in fine weather, the plant was sometimes called 'Shepherd's Clock'.

Bees just love this alkanet, Anchusa capensis, 'Blue Angel'.

Anchusa   Bees just love this alkanet, *Anchusa capensis*. The intense blue of 'Blue Angel' is wonderful at the front of a summer border. The purple 'Blue Bird' is, at about 50 cm, twice as tall, and 'Dawn' flowers in a mixture of pink, white, blue and lavender.

Anethum   Dill is not only a herb, the leaves of which are delicious with new potatoes and fish, but it has such beautiful yellow-green umbellifers that the plant is worth a place in the border.
Dill is lovely for bouquets. *Anethum graveolens* var. *hortorum* 'Vierling' is a special selection available from some seed merchants and garden centres.

Antirrhinum   There are tall, medium and dwarf snapdragons, *Antirrhinum majus*, in all sorts of colours. The most beautiful colours have been brought together in the 'Tip Top' mixture that reaches 80-100 cm. Antirrhinums from the 'Butterfly'-series are even double!

Opposite page: the rustling white flowers of the winged everlasting, Ammobium alatum 'Bikini', have a yellow centre.

Anyone preferring a colour-harmonising border could choose 'The Rose', 'Ruby', 'Snowflake' or the well-known 'Black Prince'. The medium height (50 cm) antirrhinums from the 'Coronette'-series also fit in the border.

A meadow full of dill, Anethum graveolens var. hortorum 'Vierling', to use in bouquets.

45

Antirrhinum majus
nanum *'Tahiti Mixed'*
is a low antirrhinum
for in a pot or bed.

The situation is different with the very low antirrhinums. These dwarfs, which try to hold their heads high in order to look a little bit like a snapdragon, do well in pots. They are for sale in the 'Tahiti'-series, mixed or in a single colour. If antirrhinums behave like wall-flowers and nestle in the pointing of a garden wall, they will be perennials.

Argyranthemum
'Mawl', is a change
from a white shrub
marguerite.

Argyranthemum

The well-known shrub marguerite *Argyranthemum frutescens* belongs to the plants produced from cuttings and can be kept through the winter as a tub plant. It is a rewarding plant and is usually grown in pots. Deadheading extends the flowering period. The white shrub marguerite is the most well known, but there are also pink and yellow varieties. These are usually not sold by name, but by colour. The double cultivars look rather like chrysants. Some growers do stock them under name: 'Vancouver', a double pink, 'Rosalinde', a small-flowered pink, and 'Yellow Star', a large-flowered soft yellow.

Asperula

All of a sudden everyone had blue woodruff, *Asperula orientalis (Asperula azurea),* in their gardens. It seemed to be something completely new, but, as so often happens, this is a plant which has existed for a long time and has been re-discovered. It grows wild in the cornfields of Syria and Lebanon. This 30 cm tall plant likes a spot in partial shade. The blue flowers have a delicious fragrance. Christopher Lloyd remarked that it was high time to select from this plant because some are faded blue. Some nurseries have 'Sebosa' as plant and others as seed.

Atriplex Orache, *Atriplex hortensis,* you would expect to find this in the vegetable garden. The young leaves of this relation of spinach are delicious in salad. But in the border it is used to give a restful effect. Once you have it in your garden you will never need to sow it again – it will take care of that itself. The plants grow to more than 1 metre. Usually the red orache is grown, but if you plant 'Rubra', 'Purpurea', 'Red Plume' or 'Cupreata', it does not mean that these will appear. They will in any case have red leaves. It is best to select for yourself by removing all oraches before they make seed, except those that have the most beautiful coloured leaves. 'Gold Plume' has yellow leaves and 'Green Plume' has green leaves.

Begonia The small, colourful begonias from seed, *Begonia semperflorens,* really can't help the fact that they don't fit into the image of a modern border. But that does not prevent them from flowering profusely and they are frequently used in pots and beds. They can be sown at home but need a lot of warmth. There are a great many series, such as the Ascot, Early Globe and the Olympia. They come in white, pink, red, salmon, even bicoloured and with a choice of green or brown leaves.

Blue woodruff, Asperula orientalis, *thrives in partial shade.*

Below left: orache, Atriplex hortensis, *thrives not only in the vegetable garden, but also in the border. Below right:* Begonia semperflorens, *are rewarding pot plants, but are difficult to sow indoors.*

Bellis   The genuine daisy, *Bellis perennis,* has a number of large-flowered biennial relations which flower in early spring. 'Monstruosus' has the largest flowers and 'Pomponette' has flowers like buttons. The seeds are usually on sale as mixtures, but the red, pink and white seeds can be bought separately. *Bellis perennis* 'Kito' has cherry-coloured buttons. 'Pomponette' combines well with grape hyacinths. Sow in July for flowering in the following year. *Bellis rotundifolia* is only 10 cm high and has soft lilac-coloured flowers.

The cheerful yellow stars of Bidens ferulifolia *are beautiful in border and pot.*

Bidens   *Bidens ferulifolia* used to be known as *Coreopsis.* The cheerful yellow flowers look like those of the perennial. By its loose manner of growth, the fine leaves and large bright yellow flowers, the plant is suitable for the border. 'Golden Goddess', like the species, tolerates bad weather well and both will happily go on flowering.

Brachyscome   With or without "s"? Opinions still differ on this, but *Brachyscome* or *Brachycome* – who cares! The lovely flowers of both the annual plant derived from seed *Brachyscome iberidifolia* and the plant produced from cuttings *Brachyscome multifida* do not flower the less for this. The plants originally come from Australia. Their only requirement is a lot of sun. *Brachyscome iberidifolia* can be sown as a mixture, but it is more fun to sow 'Blue Splendour', 'Purple Splendour' and 'White Splendour' by colour. In this way the 25 cm tall plants can be nicely

Page opposite: Bellis perennis *'Pomponette'. The biennial cultivated daisy has larger flowers than its wild sister.*

combined. *Brachyscome multifida* is very often used for hanging baskets and is rewarding and long-flowering. The varieties 'Amethyst' and 'Break O'Day' are available from some growers.

Brassica   Since the 'potagers' have become popular again, the ornamental cabbage has also returned. They look rather strange, these unusually shaped and coloured cabbages. The cooler their position, the more beautiful the colour. Therefore, don't sow them until early summer. These 'autumn flowers' can be found in Thompson & Morgan's catalogue, not under the "B" of *Brassica*, but under the "F" for Flowering Cabbage and Kale. The ornamental cabbages such as those from the 'Northern Light Series' and 'Osaka Red & White' have the real, round cabbage shape with a white, red or pink heart. The bizarre ornamental cabbages of the kale-type, 'Red & White Peacock', are more pointed with fernlike green leaves and have a white heart (those with the dark red leaves have a pink heart). 'White Sparrow' looks very out of the ordinary.

Briza   Of the three species of quaking grass, *Briza maxima, Briza media* and *Briza minima*, the first and last are annuals. The tall quaking grass, *Briza maxima* (50 cm), is a very decorative grass with pendulous flowers. It is not only excellent for drying; it also mixes well with other annuals and perennials. The small quaking grass *Briza minor*,

The bizarre ornamental cabbage 'White Sparrow'. It looks as though the sparrows have been at it.

is only half the size and has much smaller flowers. It is useful to re-serve a corner in the vegetable garden for the most delicate drying flowers.

Tall quaking grass,
Briza maxima, *subtly combined with white Californian poppy.*

Bupleurum *Bupleurum rotundifolium,* thorow-wax, a no-problem plant with the inflorescense of the *Euphorbia* and leaves like the *Eucalyptus,* has become a real success. When the plant was introduced, years ago, there was little interest for it, but it is now often used in mixed bou-quets.

Thorow-wax, which is also an adventive wild plant, looks just as if the stalk grows straight through the leaves. This is because the leaves completely enclose the stalk. An ideal plant, about 60 cm high, for weaving into the border.

Calceolaria The slippers cannot agree with each other: are they indoor plants or bedding plants? Did they do their best to make their slippers as big and colourful as possible, only to have those common yellow slippers steal the show?

The plants for pots or beds with the oversized slippers were really only suitable for a Victorian flowerbed. Everyone had written them off, until suddenly that little slipper flower *Calceolaria mexican* came onto the scene and so did the cultivated annual *Calceolaria integri-folia.*

Calceolaria integrifolia, *the modest slippers combined with* Lilium *'Connecticut King'.*

51

Both fit into the border and can even be picked. Let us hope that the improvers do not blow these species up to large cultivars. There is already a *Calceolaria integrifolia* 'Goudboeket'.

Summer aster, Callistephus chinensis 'Duchess Formule Mix', is not a make of racing car – but has all its allures!

Calendula

Dwarf marigolds are often seen in pots, in the border. There are countless species: single, double, cactus-flower, with flowers ranging in colour from light lemon-yellow to apricot.

A lot of tinkering has gone on with the *Calendula officinalis* and sometimes it is difficult to get hold of the ordinary single variety. Fortunately, they are still available. Dwarf marigolds, some of which, like *Calendula officinalis*, only grow to 25 cm, are of course eminently suitable for pots.

Graham Rice thinks these are 'out of character', however. He prefers the taller cultivars, such as 'Indian Prince', 'Radio' and 'Apricot Beauty', which can be beautifully worked into borders and bouquets. Thompson & Morgan have a yellow, single, silver-leaved marigold, *Calendula muselli*.

Dwarf double marigolds.

Callistephus

Summer asters, *Callistephus chinensis*, are fun but troublesome. From the moment they are sown they are extremely sensitive to damping off and in order to prevent wilt you have to plant them in a different place in the garden each year.

This typical vegetable garden flower used to rotate with the other crops. For cut flowers the taller varieties are the most suitable.

The large pink and blue bells in this bouquet are 'Canterbury Bells', Campanula medium.

Campanula　Many campanulas are perennials, but the Canterbury bells, *Campanula medium*, and chimney bell flowers, *Campanula pyramidalis*, are biennials. The former can reach 1 metre and the latter a stunning 2 metres.

Canterbury bells can be single, double or 'cup and saucer' varieties. This 'Calycanthema' has large sepals, which are like a saucer under a petal cup and are the same colour.

The seed can be bought by colour; a new pink variant is 'Russian Pink'. The Chimney Bell flowers have impressive star-shaped flowers on tall stalks.

These plants often used to be grown indoors in pots. The reason for this was that flowers pollinated by bees, wilt within four days, whereas unpollinated flowers stay beautiful for a good four weeks. That is why they were grown as pot plants and brought inside as soon as they started to flower.

Centaurea　The real cornflower is, of course, blue. The cultivar which comes closest to this colour is *Centaurea cyanus* 'Blue Diadem'. This tall cornflower is beautiful in bouquets and borders, just like the dark purple

The 'genuine' cornflower Centaurea cyanus *'Diadem' is blue.*

53

'Black Boy', the red 'Red Boy', the pink 'Pinkie' and the white 'Snow-man'. The low white 'Snowball' and the cornflowers from the Flor-ence-series are better for pots. The mixture 'Frosted Queen' even has bicoloured petals.

Cheiranthus   Wallflowers, *Cheiranthus cheiri,* should really grow on a wall. In the garden these biennials are often combined with tulips. The deliciously fragrant wallflowers must be sown at the end of May in order to form a sturdy plant before the winter.
Yellow, brown and red are the main colours. 'Fair Lady' is a mixture of pastel colours. A number of wallflowers are now included in the genus *Erysimum.*

Chrysanthemum   Only a few species of annual belong to the genus *Chrysanthemum.* Even the 'real' chrysant is now called *Dendranthema. Chrysanthe-mum carinatum,* the ox-eye daisy, reaches 50-60 cm. 'Poolster' has white flowers with a yellow ring and a dark centre. The 'Court Jesters' mixture is very cheerful. *Chrysanthemum coronarium* is from 50 cm in a primula colour 'Primrose Gem', but also in a golden-yellow shade 'Golden Gem'. *Chrysanthemum segetum,* the yellow corn marigold, which still appears here and there in the wild, has 'Prado', 'Eastern Star' and 'Eldorado' as cultivars, they are all yellow with a dark ring in the centre.

Wallflowers + forget-me-nots = springtime.

Chrysanthemum multicaule is a low plant, nice for planters, etc. 'Moonlight' has lemon-yellow flowers.

Chrysanthemum paludosum looks like the *C. multicaule,* but has white flowers with a yellow centre. 'Cecilia' and 'Annette', ideal flowers for cutting, originated through cross-matching *C. coronarium* and *C. segetum.*

Cladanthus   *Cladanthus arabicus* is an unusual plant with golden-yellow flowers and bright green, fine leaves. Because the plant makes new side-shoots under each flower, which in turn do the same when they bloom, a sturdy plant is formed – height and width 50 cm.

Clarkia   *Clarkia unguiculata (C. elegans)* is the old-fashioned clarkia which used to grace the beds with its peppermint-rock colours. The seed can be bought by colour, 'Albatross' (white), 'Apple Blossom' (apricot) and as a mixture of various colours. These mixed clarkias combine excellently with the charming 'Flash' or 'Fantasia' mixtures of the *Iberis,* which have the same colours. *Clarkia pulchella* has finely incised petals, which gives this 30-40 cm tall plant a somewhat airier appearance.

Clarkia breweri, the shortest of the clarkias, has unusually shaped flowers. Nowadays godetias are often called clarkias, but here we discuss them separately.

Clarkia pulchella, *a mixture of double and semi-double flowers.*

Clarkia. an old-fashioned cut flower.

Next page: Convolvulus tricolor *'Dark Blue', a cheerful flower with a yellow and white centre.*

55

Cleome   *Cleome hassleriana,* the spider flower, is one of the most impressive summer flowers. The spider effect is a result of the long, protruding stamens. They steal the show until far into autumn and it seems as if they will never stop blooming. The flowers open from the bottom up. After flowering they form long, slender pods, which stick out just like the stamens. Small wonder that the cultivars are all named 'Queen'. All the queens together, 'Cherry Queen', Pink Queen', White Queen', 'Purple Queen', 'Violet Queen' and 'Rose Queen', form the mixture 'Colour Fountain'. *Cleome serrulata* is shorter and the colours are not as bright.

Cathedral bells, Cobaea scandens, *is an annual climber.*

Left: the spider flower, Cleome hassleriana, *gets its name through its stamens.*

Cobaea   Cathedral Bells, a climbing plant cultivated as an annual, because it does not survive the winter, comes in two colours. *Cobaea scandens* is, according to Christopher Lloyd, murky purple, while others call it violet. They will surely agree on the colour of *Cobaea scandens* 'Alba': white. In one summer this plant can reach a respectable height and then requires a lot of watering.

Collinsia   Just like the slightly shorter *Collinsia grandiflora, Collinsia hetero-phylla (C. bicolor)* has bicoloured flowers, forming a wreath around the stalk. The first one has lilac-blue flowers, while the second has white with violet. It is one of the few summer flowers which tolerates shade.

Convolvulus   *Convolvulus tricolor (C. minor)* is a striking plant with blue, pink or white flowers with a white centre. This morning glory is fortunately not only available as a mixture but also in blue; it would be otherwise a very variegated whole. 'Blue Ensign', 'Blue Tilt', 'Blue Flash' and 'Dark Blue' are – as can be expected – blue. 'Rose Ensign' is pink and 'White Ensign' white. *Convolvulus sabaticus* is an extremely attractive plant produced from cuttings, often used in pots and hanging baskets. *Convolvulus cneorum,* also produced from cuttings, is actually a shrub, but does very well in a large pot.

Both the genuine annual golden coreopsis, Coreopsis tinctoria, *and this perennial species,* Coreopsis grandiflora, *are cultivated as annuals.*

Coreopsis   The annual, golden coreopsis, *Coreopsis tinctoria,* is often on sale as a mixture, such as 'Dwarf Mixed', with yellow, yellow and brown, and brown-red blooms 30-40 cm tall. Many golden coreopsis are bi-coloured, often yellow with a brown-red ring. 'Carmen' has single, brown-red flowers. *Coreopsis grandiflora* is usually cultivated as an annual. The double 'Early Sunrise' and 'Sunray' have yellow flowers and actually differ only in flowering season.

Cosmos   If there is one plant suitable for planting between border plants, then it is the cosmea. The pink, white and purple shades are still the nicest, although yellow and orange are also available now. Christopher Lloyd of Great Dixter hasn't a good word for the latter – they don't do well in his garden. *Cosmos bipinnatus* has many cultivars, on sale

Cosmos bipinnatus *'Sea Shells' is a sturdy shrub which brightens the garden up with flowers until the autumn.*

as mixtures, but also by colour. Unusual cultivars are 'Sea Shells', with the petals forming tubes, and 'Daydream', with white petals running into pink towards the centre. 'Candy Stripe' is pink-edged. 'Trianon' is crimson-red and 'Versailles Tetra' is lilac-purple. The white 'Sonata' is not as tall, but at 60 cm it still makes a good flower for cutting.

Hawk's beard, Crepis rubra, *is also available in white.*

Crepis   Hawk's beard, actually a very ordinary flower 40 cm tall, combines well with other plants. The pink *Crepis rubra* goes beautifully with grey-leaved plants. The white hawk's beard 'Snow white' or 'Snow plume', is just like the pink hawk's beard, a good cut flower.

Cucurbita   Not a summer flower, but summer fruits, or even better, autumn fruits. Large and small decorative gourds are very attractive against an arch, over the compost heap or along a fence. In particular the bottle gourd (not *Cucurbita* but *Lagenaria*) is extremely decorative. Ornamental gourds, *Cucurbita pepo* 'Ovifera', are easy to grow and very varied in shape and colour. After harvesting they are still beautiful in a row on the windowsill. Crowns are decorative gourds on which the stiffened bloom petals look liked reversed crowns. The smaller edible pumpkins can also be trained well over arches and fences, although the leaves are somewhat coarser. 'Sweet Dumpling', 'Jack be Little' and 'Turks Turban' are also very decorative.

Pumpkins are annual and well worth the trouble of cultivating.

Cuphea *Cuphea lanceolata* and *Cuphea ignea (platycentra)* is known as cigar plant. The bright red flowers do look rather like a cigar.
Cuphea lavea var. miniata even has a scarlet cultivar called 'Firefly'. This 30 cm tall plant does well in pots, beds or border. The long flowering season makes it excellent for combining with the autumn-flowering *Sedum spectabile.*
Cuphea lanceolata grows to a height of 65 cm and *Cuphea viscosissima* reaches 50 cm.

The cigar plant,
Cuphea ignea,
is back!

Cynoglossum Anyone who has these Chinese forget-me-nots in the garden doesn't want to lose them. *Cynoglossum amabile* – also known as hound's tongue – has magnificent blue cultivars. 'Firmament' and 'Blue Bird' are much the same with their sky-blue flowers. 'Blue Shower' is taller (60-70 cm), flowers more profusely and fits beautifully in mixed borders and bouquets.
'Pink Shower' is the pink little sister, 'Avalanche' is, as the name suggests, white. 'Mystery Rose', white flowers with a pink blush, is new and does very well in a pink border.

Hound's tongue or Chinese forget-me-not, Cynoglossum, *is a good border and bouquet plant.*

Dahlia   The big advantage (or disadvantage) of sowing dahlias from seed is that after the growing season you can relegate them to the compost heap and you are not stuck with the tubers the whole winter. Dahlia seeds are almost always sold as mixtures. If there are particularly nice ones among them, it is possible to keep these and grow them on the next year. The plants of the 'Redskin' series have dark leaves. 'Unwin Dwarf Hybrids' is a cheerful mixture and there are also white-flowered dahlias 'Mignon Silver', *Dahlia coccinea* and a colourful mixture of single dahlias.

Dahlias can also be sown.

Delphinium   Annual larkspur is no longer called *Delphinium*, but *Consolida*. Not everyone is used to this though, so we have used the old name here. There are two sorts of annual larkspur, the rocket bouquet-larkspur, *Delphinium ajacis (Consolida ambigua)*, which is hardly branched, and the strongly branching larkspur, *Delphinium consolida (Consolida regalis)*.

The annual variety is usually known as larkspur. The perennial delphinium, *D. consolida* is mostly used for cut flowers and for drying. 'Blue Cloud' has beautiful single, dark blue flowers and is strongly branched. 'Frosted Skies' grows to 1 metre and has large, white blue-edged flowers. 'White Spire' is the best white and 'Exquisite Rose' is a beautiful pink. There are also various tall and shorter mixtures of both sorts. The flowers dry well.

Annual larkspurs, Delphinium ajacis (Consolida ambigua), *are beautiful in bouquets, whether fresh or dried.*

Dianthus   Of the annual (and annual cultivated) carnations, the *Dianthus hybrida* 'Colour Magician' is a very strange one: it has different coloured flowers on one plant. *Dianthus chinensis* 'Raspberry Parfait' and 'Strawberry Parfait' are those colourful little carnation clumps, which are retarded and put on the market as bedding plants. The beautiful carnation *Dianthus superbus,* has a more natural manner of growth. It is a short-lived perennial, which is cultivated as an annual. The flowers of this species are lilac-pink and deeply fringed. The cultivars 'Red Feather' and 'White Feather' flower more profusely and are a little taller (40-45 cm). Sweet William, *Dianthus barbatus,* has been a best-seller for years.

This biennial is usually cultivated mixed. but is also sold by colour. The higher specimens are very suitable for cutting and it is a very good idea to combine a later-flowering cultivar such as 'Crimson Velvet' with other plants.

Diascia   Honest growers say that it is an annual, others put it among the perennials. *Diascia* is a perennial from South Africa, but is grown here as an annual because it is not hardy. As a rare exception a plant may survive a mild winter, but do not rely on this.

It is best to take 5-10 cm long cuttings in August/September. Cut them off at a joint; because the stalk is hollow between the joints and the cutting would rot. It is possible, of course, to sow the plant each year.

Next page:
Sweet Williams,
Dianthus barbatus,
combine splendidly
with papavers.

Dianthus hybrida
'Colour Magician', a
carnation with differ-
ent colours on one
plant.

Diascia barberae and the cultivars 'Rubra', 'Pink Queen' and 'Ruby Field' are quite common as is the species *Diascia rigescens,* which is slightly taller (50 cm).

The colour spectrum of the diascias moves through pink, salmon and orange. The profusely-flowering plants are not only good in pots, but can also be combined with perennials.

Didiscus   *Didiscus coeruleus* is also known as *Trachymene coerulea.* The blue lace flower from Australia has a somewhat spherical inflorescence on long stems, by which the flower rather resembles the scabius. The soft-blue flowers fit very well in a border. They are also good cut flowers. The plants grow to 60 cm.

Digitalis   *Digitalis purpurea,* the common foxglove, is an attractive plant. There are also beautiful cultivars of this biennial. 'Alba', the white one is not so far away from its ancestors, because pure white flowers are also found in the wild. In catalogues you mostly find the mixture 'Excelsior-Hybrids'. This impudent foxglove is not everyone's cup of tea.

This new generation looks you straight in the eye, because the flowers grow all round the stems and are almost horizontal. *Digitalis ferruginea* is a magnificent foxglove, 1.5 metres tall with orchid-like yellow-

Diascia rigescens *supported by* stachys.

brown flowers. An 'architectural' plant, which sometimes flowers for an extra year.

Dimorphoteca   Botanists have fiddled about quite a bit with *Dimorphoteca* and *Osteospermum*. We seem to have given up trying to differentiate between them, and now call everything *Osteospermum*. The difference appears to be that the disc florets of *Dimorphoteca* do not make seed – the *Osteospermum* disc florets and the ray flowers both make seed. This information does not help you much when you are looking something up in a catalogue, though. These South-African flowers, which open only in sunny weather, are none the less cheerful for this. *Dimorphoteca sinuata* 'Goliath' has 30-40 cm high orange flowers, which are good for cutting and look splendid in a red border. *Dimorphoteca pluvialis* 'Pole Star' and 'Glistening White' can be found in Thompson & Morgan's catalogue under the osteopermums.

Dipsacus   Dipsacus fullonum, the large common teasel, is very rarely found in the wild now. Since it is forbidden to pick protected plants, we sow this biennial ourselves. For this plant the following applies: once you have teasels you have them forever. Weeding them out where you don't want them is the solution. The lilac-coloured flowers start to bloom in a circle around the teasel and bloom top and bottom at the same time, to the enjoyment of bees and butterflies. Goldfinches like

The tall teasels, Dipsacus fullonum, *are a jewel for every high border.*

Dimorphoteca *nowadays known as* Osteospermum.

the seeds. Through their airy way of growth the tall teasels (up to 2 metres) fit in any border. Don't clear them out before the winter, because they are beautiful in the snow too.

A colourful combination of cosmos, nicotiana and petunias.

Dolichos The lablab, a climbing bean, is a remarkable vegetable, grown more for its flowers than for the edible pods, seeds and even the roots. The lablab has to be sown indoors with heat and not planted out until the ground has warmed up, because it is a real sun worshipper. In warm regions in America the plant is grown instead of sweet peas. The scented flowers look like those of the wisteria, only they are not pendulous but stand erect.

The purple, red or white flowers stand out beautifully against the dark leaves. This plant can be trained over an arch beautifully. *Dolichos lablab* 'ruby Moon' has purple flowers. Thompson & Morgan has the species.

Dorotheanthus Formerly *Mesembryanthemum*, now *Dorotheanthus bellidiformis*. These Livingstone daisies come from South-Africa, where, at Ysterfontein, they shine in the sun. It must be a wonderful sight to see all those colourful little faces like dandelions on the edge of the road. They only open when the sun shines and these children of the sun do not like wet feet either.

Do not plant them in the same place every year. In a good mixture

68

there are pink, salmon-colour, apricot, yellow and white flowers. 'Pastel Mixture' is a subtle mix of only pastel shades, 'Lunette' is light yellow with a red eye.

Echium plantagineum *'Light Blue Bedder', a sky-blue cultivar.*

Eccremocarpus   *Eccremocarpus scaber*, glory vine, a perennial climber, is grown as an annual, because (with a few exceptions) it does not survive our winters. This plant, which can reach a height of 4 metres, must be sown indoors. The tubular flowers, which are in large bunches, are orange with yellow.

They are not only sold as a mixture, 'Tresco Mixture', 'Anglia Hybrids' or 'Fireworks', but also by colour.

'Tresco Gold' and 'Aureus' are yellow, 'Tresco Rose' is dark-pink and 'Tresco Scarlet' is orange-red. The plants are very suitable for climbing through shrubs.

Left: Eccremocarpus scaber, *an annual cultivated climber, is beautiful if allowed to climb through shrubs.*

Echium   Viper's bugloss, *Echium plantagineum,* has a wild cousin, *Echium vulgare,* found in the dunes. The cultivars of the cultivated species are shorter (30 cm). The mixtures of this plant, 'Bedding Mixed', 'Bedder Mixture' and 'T&M Dwarf Mixed', surprise us with all shades of blue, pink and white.

The bees enjoy them just as much as we do. 'Blue Bedder' and 'Light Blue Bedder' are single coloured. The latest cultivated one is sky-blue. The plant seeds itself.

Next page:

Erigeron Opinions differ about *Erigeron karvinskianus* 'Profusion'. This particularly attractive plant, that comes into bloom within three months of sowing and only stops when the frosts come, can seed itself to such an extent that it almost becomes a weed.

In a mild winter the plants prove that they are actually perennials. These are the plants with their soft pink to white daisies that seed themselves between the steps in the garden. They love walls too. They hang over pots and hanging baskets and mingle with the plants in the border. Why do we immediately think that everything that is doing well is a weed?

Erigeron karvinskianus 'Profusion' likes to seed itself. The daisy-like flowers are growing here together with Corydalis ochroleuca on a wall.

Erysimum Some wallflowers are no longer named *Cheiranthus* but *Erysimum* and are then called Siberian wallflowers. The most well-known of these is the orange *Erysimum x allionii* 'Orange Bedder', which blooms about the end of April. These biennials have to be sown in June or July of the previous year. 'Glassnost Mixed' is a mixture of pastel colours. The lilac-pink 'Bowles Mauve' can't be found in a seed catalogue, because this sterile plant can only be propagated by cuttings, just as the soft-yellow 'Moonlight'. *Erysimum linifolium* with silver-grey foliage and blue-purple flowers can be sown.

Eschscholtzia The genuine Californian poppy, *Eschscholtzia californica*, should be orange. But, because the bright colour of 'Orange King', for example, did not fit in so well in our harmonious and softly-tinted gardens, many cultivars in other colours have come onto the market. The crimson-red 'Rose Bush', white 'Milky White', red 'Dalli' and lilac-pink 'Purple Gleam' are a little more modest.

Mixtures are 'Mission Bells', with tiny rosettes in all colours and semi-double blooms, and 'Thai Silk', with pleated petals and bright colours.

To protect their pollen, Californian poppies only open in fine weather. Orange Californian poppy with bright red Papaver commutatum 'Ladybird' make a daring combination.

Euphorbia marginata 'White Top', a foliage plant which is very suitable for bouquets.

Euphorbia   Annual euphorbias generally do not feel at home in this climate as well as the perennial species. But it is worth trying to grow the variegated *Euphorbia marginata* 'Early Snow', 'White Top' or 'Late Snow' between colourful annuals. The plants reach 60-90 cm high and have greyish-green and white leaves – beautiful to use as green foliage in bouquets. The plants contain milk; therefore, after picking, cut off the stalks to length under water or sear them in a candle flame for a moment.

A colourful mix of Californian poppies, Eschscholtzia californica, on a sunny day.

Felicia   *Felicia amelloides* can be sown or propagated by cuttings. The 50-60 cm tall plants have bright blue flowers with a yellow centre, and look very nice in pots. The cultivars 'Reads Blue' and 'Santa Anita' only

reach 30 cm. There is also a white and a variegated cultivar. *Felicia amoena* is also in blue, white and variegated. Variegated refers to the leaves and not to the flowers. Christopher Lloyd hasn't a good word to say for 'Kingfisher Daisy', *Felicia bergeriana*. He calls this species a 'rotten little annual', that only opens on sunny mornings. It probably rained a lot in his garden at that time. Anyway, the other blue daisies are not bothered by this. They are certainly well worth the trouble.

This fuchsia cannot be sown, but has to be grown from cuttings.

Fuchsia   Fuchsias are not annuals and are not cultivated as such. They are tub plants. They are mentioned here because nowadays there are fuchsias which can be grown from seed. 'Florabelle' won a gold medal in 1995. This well-branching plant flowers 14 weeks after sowing, with semi-double purple and red flowers. They should be sown in January, in a warm place. Thompson & Morgan has the 'Chimes Mixed' mixture with all kinds of goodies: single, double, hanging and standing fuchsias.

Gaillardia   The cockade flower originally comes from America, where it is called 'Blanket Flower', because it has the same colours as the Indians' blankets. Of the annual *Gaillardia pulchella* we usually see the bicoloured flowers of *G. pulchella var. picta*. 'Crimson Giant' (90 cm) has single flowers, varying in colour from dark red to dark brown, with

The cockade Gaillardia pulchella *with double yellow blooms:* 'Yellow Plume'

yellow marking at the edge. 'Lorenza Lollipop' is a low, double mixture in all shades of red and yellow. 'New Pastels' has rather softer pastel shades. 'Red Plume' and 'Yellow Plume' are single-coloured and have double flowers looking like pompons.

Pots full of summer flowers in a cheerful arrangement.

Gazania Gazanias, from South-Africa, are usually on sale as mixtures, such as 'Chansonette', 'Sunshine Mixture' or 'Mini-Star Mixed'. The F1-hybrids of 'Sundance Mixed' look bizarre with their contrasting stripe on each petal.
They are good cut flowers and therefore it is better to grow them in a corner of the vegetable garden than in the border. 'Ministar White' has shiny dark-green leaves and white, star-shaped flowers. These rather 'wooden soldiers' are a little difficult to fit in, but they are rewarding performers in pots.

Gazania 'Ministar Mixed'

Gilia We find many annuals among the gilias, but here too a very confusing change of name is going on. Many of what used to be known as *Gilia* are now known as *Leptosiphon, Linanthus* or *Ipomopsis. Gilia tricolor* has solitary flowers with three or four colourful rings, from yellow in the centre to purple in the middle and soft blue at the edge. These flowers, which smell of chocolate, do well in the perennial border. 'Snow Queen' is a white selection. *Gilia capitata,* 'Queen Anne's thimbles', is 30-60 cm tall and has blue flowers, which stand together in large bunches. This species fits excellently into a cottage garden. Sow in April/May in the place where it is to flower, or in the autumn for early flowering.

Godetia   Even Gertrude Jekyll mixed these into her borders – the double ones! There are still: 'Double White', 'Double Nain Cherie Sweetheart' and 'T&M Tall Double Mixed'.
The single godetias are more refined. They can be bought by colour. 'Sybil Sherwood' is light pink with a white edge, 'Memoria' is white, 'Aurora' salmon-coloured, 'Furora' deep red and 'Lilac Lady' has very beautiful mauve flowers. Godetias and clarkias look very alike and in the *Index of Garden Plants* all godetias are called clarkias. But since the Godetia is mentioned in all catalogues as a separate genus, we do the same here.

Gomphrena   The globe amaranth is actually an everlasting flower, but the plant is certainly worth a place in the border. The modest clover-like round flower-heads fit in excellently with other annuals and perennials in the border. They are available by colour or mixed. 'Professor Plum' – which does honour to its name –, the white 'Innocence' and the pink 'Blushing Bride' are 60 cm tall. *Gomphrena haageana* 'Aurantiaca' is 80 cm tall and light orange. Sow globe amaranths in March in a warm place and plant them outside in May-June. They love sun. If you want

Is Clarkia bottiae *'Pink Joy' a godetia after all, do you think?*

to dry them, pick the flower-heads just before they open. There are also dwarf varieties for sale as pot plants. These 'Rosalinde', 'Buddy' and 'Bianca' are not suitable for drying.

The annual Gypsophila elegans *can already be sown in the autumn.*

Gypsophila

The annual gypsophila belies its fragile appearance and can already be sown outside even in the autumn . *Gypsophila elegans* 'Snow Fountain' and 'White Monarch' have slightly larger white flowers, 'Rosea' has pink flowers, 'Carminea' is crimson-pink and 'Kermesina' crimson-red.

Because of their height (60-70 cm) they form beautiful wispy clouds between other annuals and perennials. Good for picking, although you cannot beat the perennial gypsophila as cut flower. The pot trend has brought *Gypsophila muralis* back again. This creeping gyp is only 15-20 cm tall. 'Garden Bride' is pink and 'Gypsy' has double pink flowers.

Helianthus

Is there anyone who doesn't know them, the sunflowers? *Helianthus annuus,* the sovereign among the summer flowers. 'Lemon Queen' with lime-yellow flowers, 'Bronze King' with brown flowers and 'Velvet Queen' with flowers of dark crimson, grow to a height of 1.5 metres. The height varies from the gigantic 'Uniflorus Giganteus' and 'Russian Giant' to the compact dwarfs 'Teddy Bear' and 'Sunspot'. Dwarfs in pots are not always natural dwarfs, but are often kept small

Next page:
the cockade flower
Gaillardia pulchella
with double red flowers: 'Red Plume'.

Helichrysum bracte-
atum *'hot Bikini', a*
dried flower which
grows to 50 cm.

with retardants. The very tall sunflowers need support. Graham Rice suggests letting a *Thunbergia alata* climb up the stick and the plant. 'Colour Fashion' is good for picking and *Helianthus debilis* 'Italian White' is the most beautiful white sunflower.

Helichrysum

'The' everlasting flower, *Helichrysum bracteatum*, is often on sale as a mixture. 'Monstruosum' is 1 metre tall and comprises the genuine colours of the immortelles: yellow, brown, pink and white. 'Pastel Mixed' goes better in the border with its pastel shades. 'Silvery Rose' and 'Frosted Silver' have subtle misty yellow and pink colours. The brightly-coloured immortelles keep their colours better than these pastel ones. 'Bikini' is a shorter version (40-50 cm). These straw skirts are on sale mixed or by colour.

Helichrysum cassianum is a fine pink immortelle, with 'Gabriel Pink' and 'Lichtrosa' as cultivars. *Helichrysum subulifolium* has masses of bright-yellow flowers, which dry very well because of their strong stems (40 cm). *Helichrysum* also has 'summer foliage'.

Helichrysum petiolare is a non-hardy shrub, propagated through cuttings and excellent for pots and containers. The decorative branches show up well, either hanging or creeping. There are various cultivars with a yellow, light-grey or even variegated colour. 'Silver', 'Silver Bush', 'Yellow' and 'Limelight' have leaf colour indicated by their names.

Helichrysum petiolare
'Silver Bush' with silver-coloured foliage,
a plant derived from
cuttings, which combines fantastically
with summer flowers.

Opposite page:
the lime-yellow sunflower Helianthus
annuus 'Lemon
Queen'.

Heliotropium   Heliotrope can be grown from cuttings or sown. It is actually a shrub which also belongs to the tub plants because it can be kept through the winter. The early-flowering violet-blue 'Early Violet' and 'Early Blues' smell like 'Cherry Pie' as the plant is sometimes called. It is a somewhat 'stiff' plant, suitable for pots and beds enclosed by box hedging, combined with *Plectranthus,* another plant to grow from cuttings, which, with its variegated leaves, creeps around and does credit to the dark heliotrope.

Helipterum   A modest immortelle, looking a little like the *Helichrysum bracteatum,* but smaller and only in pink and white. *Helipterum roseum (Acrolinum)* is the most well-known (40-50 cm). It is wiser to look for cultivars by colour, because in the mixtures the white often dominates. *Helipterum manglesii (Rhodanthe)* forms small shrubs, also for planting in a pot. 'Album' (white) and 'Maculatum' (pink) both have a cheerful yellow centre. *Helipterum humboldtianum (H. sanfordii)* has larger yellow flowers and silver-grey leaves.

Hesperis   The biennial dame's violet, *Hesperis matronalis,* is often confused with honesty. However, the dame's violet has a beautiful evening scent; the honesty has not. This plant, which grows to more than 1 metre, fits in well in a perennial border. The flower clusters of this species are dark lilac, but there is a white cultivar, 'Alba'. This dame's

The deliciously sweet-smelling heliotrope Heliotropium arborescens.

violet lightens up at dusk. Sow it in summer for flowering the following year.

Iberis In addition to the well-known perennial arabis *Iberis sempervirens*, which used to brighten up everybody's garden, there are also two annual species. *Iberis amara* has flowers which are like hyacinths on a stalk. 'White Pinnacle' (50 cm) is white, just like 'Iceberg' (30 cm). 'Impudent White Spiral' is absolutely snow-white – it nearly burnt a hole in the film during a photo-session in the Botanical Gardens in Edinburgh! *Iberis umbellata* is shorter and has flatter inflorescence. 'Flash' and 'Fantasia' mixtures are fairy-tale pink, lilac, white and crimson. The seed can be bought by colour.

Iberis umbellata *has fairly flat inflorescence. The mixtures 'Fantasia', 'Flash' and 'Fairy' are particularly beautiful.*

Impatiens The improvers have swooped down on the busy lizzies with such enthusiasm that you really don't know what to choose. All seed companies have their own series, which they improve on every year. Sowing these yourself is rather difficult and requires great precision. We see this plant so much that it is a bit boring. But a couple of bright red busy lizzies are wonderful splashes of colour and a dark corner is brightened up by one or two pots of white ones. *Impatiens glandulifera* is a totally different story. This giant balsam can reach 2 m tall and, unlike its little sister, fits modestly into the border. If you don't mind the weeding, it's worth giving it a try.

Ionopsidium

Ionopsidium acaule is a ground covering plant, only 5 cm high, and blooms profusely with little mauve flowers. This miniature plant seeds itself, preferably between paving stones in the shade and blooms very early, sometimes already in the winter.

The name *Ionopsidium* literally means false violet – not a bad description, as the flowers do look a bit like violets.

Ionopsidium acaule, *a modest creeper with mauve flowers.*

Ipomoea

The ephemeral flower, *Ipomoea tricolor*, is a magnificent climber for a sunny, sheltered spot. Do not sow morning glory before mid-April and soak the seed for a short time.

Harden the plants off after sowing inside and pricking out, because they cannot stand 'stress'. Good, moist soil, a sunny spot and enough possibilities to climb are all they require. They even do well in a large pot on the balcony.

Place the pot inside a second pot or stand other pots in front, so that the sun cannot reach the roots.

The morning glory also does well in a conservatory or even in the living room.

Try letting it grow with other plants against an archway or a bush. 'Heavenly Blue' is one of the best known morning glories. *Ipomoea purpurea,* the slightly more common one is available as a mixture, but also by colour (white, pink, purple, blue).

Morning glory, Ipomoea tricolor, *a climber for a sheltered spot.*

Kochia The summer cypress is not used for its flowers but for the foliage. They really are like cypresses as they stand in the bed, chubby and spherical. The success of kochias depends on how they are positioned. All too often they are stiffly lined up, alternating with colourful annuals. It is better to put them close together so that they form a hedge, or position them in loose groups among other plants. The bright green foliage of *Kochia scoparia f. trichophylla* changes to brown-red in the autumn. 'Autumn red' does justice to its name, 'Childsii' and 'Evergreen' do not change colour, 'Acapulco Silver' has variegated foliage.

Lagurus At the end of April the hare's tail grass, *Lagurus ovatus,* can be sown outside. This grass usually comes in a mixture of decorative grasses, but can be obtained separately. The species can reach 40-60 cm. The cultivar 'Bunny Tails' is 20 cm, very uniform and, because of its height, more suitable to use between other annuals. It is suitable for picking and drying.

Lantana Lantanas are real plants-from-cuttings and with a bit of luck you can keep them through the winter. They are actually more suitable for tubs. They are mentioned here among the summer flowers because these cheerful plants, being of the same type as the heliotrope, can also be sown.

Lantana *can be propagated by seed or cuttings.*

This red summer cypress, Kochia scoparia, *stands a little awkwardly among the flowers. It looks better in a small group or as a hedge.*

Lathyrus *'Lilac Silk'*, *a particularly large-flowered and 'frilly' sweet pea.*

The seed is usually on sale as a mixture. Thompson & Morgan have 'Camara Mixed Hybrids', a mix of red with yellow, pink with yellow, lilac and white flowers. This sounds a little bit over-the-top, but it is always possible to take cuttings from the best ones and grow them on. These colourful plants, which change colour as they get older, attract many butterflies.

Lathyrus *'White Supreme', a beautiful pure white sweet pea.*

Lathyrus   You could fill a book about lathyrus. There are even lathyrus clubs! Every year there are exhibitions where amateur growers show their most beautiful sweet pea blooms. There are so many annual *Lathyrus odoratus* cultivars that some growers have specialised in them. Bol-tons is just one of these. Cultivars such as 'Claire Elizabeth', 'Fire-crest', 'Lilac Silk', 'Percy Thrower', 'White Supreme' and many others are described as 'highly recommended', 'sensational', 'outstanding', 'fascinating', etc.

Sweet peas combine well in the border. Trained along a tripod, a fence or over an arch, the colour of the sweet pea can play a determining role. Plant one at the foot of a bush so that the sweet pea has a natural support.

Shorter lathyrus is often available as a mixture. 'Bijou' and 'Knee-hi' can climb without support and are also suitable for pots and hanging baskets.

Lathyrus odoratus is not the only annual. Try the yellow *Lathyrus*

Left: Lathyrus *'Brian Clough', often grown for exhibitions.*

cloranthus for a change, reintroduced by Thompson & Morgan as 'Lemonade'. Or *L. tingitanus*, purple-red as species, or with all colours as a mixture.

Lathyrus does need some attention: the ground in the place where it is to stand must be dug two spades deep in the autumn, and manured. The seeds should be soaked and can be sown indoors in January and outdoors in March.

Growing lathyrus for exhibitions requires a lot of care. The more flowers you pick the better, because if the plant gets the chance to make seed, this will be at the cost of the flowers.

Next page: a white Lavatera trimestris *with large bell-shaped flowers.*

Lavatera

The annual *Lavatera trimestris* is easy to cultivate and can be sown outside where it is to flower. The sturdy plants, looking a bit like shrubs, thrive in a perennial border.

They have rather striking flowers which are close together and as big as the hibiscus flower. As far as the manner of growth is concerned, they look a bit like the stiff hibiscus bush. The white 'Mont Blanc' and 'White Regis', pink 'Silver Cup' and 'Tanagra' and dark-pink 'Ruby Regis' are good flowers for cutting.

Lavatera trimestris *'Tanagra' is a good flower for cutting.*

Legousia   *Legousia speculum-veneris,* the large Venus's looking glass, is becoming very rare and the *Legousia hybrida* has almost disappeared. Perhaps that is why we like to have it in our gardens.

'Blue Carpet' has larger flowers than the species and 'Alba' is a white cultivar. The plants are no taller than 20 cm and can be sown where they are to flower.

In order to extend the flowering period, sow several times during the summer. *Legousia pentagonica* originates from the Balkans.

Legousia pentagonica, *a very profusely-flowering Venus's looking glass from the Balkans.*

Leptosiphon   A charming little plant with delicate leaves, covered with small stars in all colours. It is only available as a mixture. This plant is well worth trying to grow, for edges, beds and between paving stones. Take 'Stardust' or 'Confetti Mixture'.

Limnanthes   At last a plant which nobody wants to improve and of which the species is obviously good enough. *Limnanthes douglasii,* the poached-egg flower, has flowers with yellow centres, a white edge and bright green leaves. The plant only reaches 15 cm but spreads and with its hundreds of flowers attracts bees. The limnanthes blooms mainly in May/early June and is very suitable for beds, pots and edging. The 'poached egg' seeds itself and the following year it only needs to be tidied up.

Right: poached-egg plant, Limnanthes douglasii, *for beds, pots and edging.*

Limonium   *Limonium sinuatum (Statice sinuata)*, the annual sea lavender, is rather stiff, compared to the perennial sea lavenders. The flowers also stick out stiffly at the top of the branched stem. Fortunately, this immortelle is not only available in a variegated mix, but also in matching pastel colours and even by colour. *Limonium sinuatum* 'Market Grower's Deep Rose' and 'Apricot Beauty' can go straight into the border with their lovely pink and apricot shades. 'Sunburst White', a large-flowered white, is for the white border, while 'Sunburst Pale Blue' and 'Market Grower's Light Blue' can go in the blue border. 'Market Grower's Yellow' and 'Sunburst Yellow' fit between yellow and red-brown flowering plants. Apart from these tall sea lavenders (75-100 cm) there are also shorter ones. *Limonium aureum* 'Sahin's Gold' (Thompson & Morgan's 'Supernova') has been rediscovered and brought back onto the market. This perennial, which is grown as a biennial yellow-gold flower, 60 cm tall, is eminently suitable as a cut flower. *Limonium suworowii* is known as *Psylliostachys* (see entry for this).

Linaria   The annual Moroccan toadflax, *Linaria maroccana,* is suitable for 'variegated beds' (says an old book). These small toadflaxes are on sale as colourful mixtures. Since they are 50-60 cm tall, they make good cut flowers. Well-known mixtures are 'Fairy Bouquet' and 'Northern Lights'. 'Antique Silver' is a cream-coloured cultivar. Much

The annual sea lavender Limonium sinuatum *'Market Grower's Light Blue'.*

more stately and stylish are the tall spikes of the perennial *Linaria purpurea*. The mauve 'Bowles Mauve', soft pink 'Canon J. Went' and white 'Alba' can also be successfully sown. These toadflaxes like to grow on a wall, if possible, just like the ivy-leaved toadflax that also used to be called *Linaria* (now *Cymbalaria muralis*).

Linum   *Linum usitatissimum*, the genuine flax for pure linen, is excellent as a blending plant in a blue border. The light-blue flowers of this delicate plant (60-90 cm) become dried flowers through their seed-boxes. 'Common Flax' has azure-blue flowers and 'Sultan's Blue' is sky-blue. Both of these are slightly shorter than the species. *Linum grandiflorum*, a large-flowered cultivated product, is 30-50 cm tall. 'Bright Eyes' has white flowers with a red centre.
The bright-red 'Rubrum' is really something special for the red border. *Linum perenne*, a perennial with larger blue flowers, can also be sown successfully.

Lobelia   Lobelias are really perennials, although they don't all survive, because they are not hardy. This explains why some lobelias, such as *Lobelia richardii*, can be propagated by cuttings. Common lobelias are those which form clumps, such as *Lobelia erinus (compacta)* and the trailing *Lobelia erinus (pendula)*.
The clumps are usually used in beds and the trailers for containers.

Flax with flowers too red to be true, Linum grandiflorum *'Rubrum'.*

White lobelias always have 10% of blue flowers, A time-consuming solution for a white border is to prick out the flowers one by one, instead of in tufts.

According to Graham Rice this formula can be successfully reversed, the trailing lobelia becoming a splendid ground cover, whereas normally in a container its shoots only dry out. Clumps can just as well be used for containers. There are so many cultivars that only the exceptional ones are given here.

'Kathleen Mallard' is a double lobelia which can only be propagated from cuttings. The vigour of this lobelia is not as strong in comparison with the others.

'Cambridge Blue' is a pretty light-blue, 'Lilac Fountain' a trailing soft-lilac cultivar. 'Blue Cascade' is a gorgeous blue trailing lobelia, 'White Lady' is white. The strange thing about white lobelias is that 10% of them are always blue, as if to remind them that they should really be blue.

Because lobelias are pricked out in tufts, the blue mixes with the white. The only way to prevent this is to prick them out one by one and sort out the white ones.

Cultivars of Lobelia x speciosa don't look like lobelias. 'Fan Scarlet' is one of these. This prizewinner has dark leaves, bright-red flowers and is 60-70 cm tall. 'Queen Victoria', also a well-known red one, looks fantastic in a red border.

'Kathleen Mallard' is a double lobelia which can only be propagated by cuttings.

Lobularia   *Alyssum*, the well-known white edging plant. Thanks to the new colours this little plant is again receiving attention.

96

In addition to the white 'Wonderland White' and 'Avalanche' and the deep-purple 'New Purple', there is now also an apricot-coloured 'New Apricot' and pink 'Rosaria' and 'Rosie O'Day'. There is even a cream-coloured 'Creamery'.

Eight harmonious colours are in the mix 'Eastern Bonnet', the colours of 'Pastel Carpet' are, of course, pastel and those of 'Wonderland Mixed' are rather bright.

Lonas   *Lonas annua (L. inodora)* is known as yellow ageratum. This easy-to-grow dried flower does have flower clusters like ageratum, but they are yellow and crackly. When all the flowers are out and the colour is at its brightest, you can pick them for drying. You can sow outside where they are to flower.

Lopezia   This modest flower is not in every catalogue. They grow to 50 cm and have clusters of pink flowers, borne at the end of the stem. The foliage brings tranquillity to a border. Proof that it is a variable plant can be found in the *Index of Garden Plants*, in which no less than 18 different *Lopezia* species are called *Lopezia racemosa* – obviously by a botanist who had had enough of it all.

Lunaria   Honesty, *Lunaria annua,* is so common that we often forget it. This 1 metre tall plant fits into the cottage garden and the border and

Lopezia racemosa *'Pretty Rose', a modest blending plant for the border.*

Lobularia maritima *'Wonderland White', the well-known edging plant.*

Next page: Malva sylvestris *'Primley Blue' is an unusual colour and reaches 40 cm.*

ensures that it is always present, by seeding itself abundantly. Not only the flowers are pretty, but also the round transparent fruits.

'Alba' and 'Sissinghurst White' are white, 'Munstead Purple' is reddish purple. There are both purple and white plants with variegated leaves.

Lupinus   Annual lupins begin to flower when the perennials have finished blooming. The nomenclature is rather confusing, but everyone agrees about *Lupinus luteus* – it is yellow.

A cultivar of this is 'Yellow Javelin'. *Lupinus nanus* (15-45 cm) has small clusters of blue and white flowers. According to the *Index* and Thompson & Morgan, the mixture 'Pixie Delight' belongs to *L. nanus*, whereas others say it should be *L. hartwegii*. They are available in blue, white and shades of pink, and are suitable for poor ground.

Lupinus texensis, the 'Texas Bluebonnet', flowers profusely with blue and white blooms.

Malope   *Malope trifida* looks very much like *Lavatera*, but is a little less stiff. Its big, tall plants (1-1.5 m) combine well in the border. They form attractive, branched shrubs which are useful for picking. The petals of malopes are narrower at the foot, allowing the green calyx to show through, which gives the effect of stained glass when the light shines

The annual lupin 'Pixie Delight' has soft colours and feels at home even on poor ground.

Malva sylvestris *(var.* mauritianus) *grows to more than a metre.*

Malva sylvestris *'Primley Blue' and a red & white Penstemon, a colourful combination of summer flowers.*

through from behind (according to Christopher Lloyd). In addition to a large-flowered mixture, there is also a crimson cultivar 'Vulcan', the white 'White Queen' with slightly smaller flowers and two pink cultivars: 'Pink Queen' and 'Rosea'.

Malva *Malva verticillata,* is actually the only real annual. The attraction of this tall plant (2 m) is not its flowers but the large, frizzy leaves. Strawberries, raspberries and wineberries look wonderful, arranged on the leaves. Sow the malva where it is to bloom.

Malva sylvestris (var. *mauritiana*), 1 to 1.5 m high, blooms from July to September with deep-purple flowers. Thompson & Morgan has the cultivar 'Bibor Felho' with larger blooms. 'Zebrina' has white-to-pink flowers veined with purple.

Malva sylvestris 'Primley Blue' has dark-veined violet-blue blooms. The plant only grows to 40 cm.

'Brave Heart' is a chance sowing, discovered by the 98-year old Sir David Scott of Boughton House and introduced by his widow after his death. It is a beautiful, lavishly-blooming tall plant with lavender-mauve darkly veined leaves.

The perennial *Malva moschata,* the musk mallow, less stiff and more decorative than *Lavatera,* comes in white – 'Alba' and 'Pirouette' – and in pink – 'Rosea' and 'Pink Perfection'.

Matthiola The most well-known, double and deliciously scented stocks are on the market as mixed or single-coloured cut flowers. If we want to grow them in the garden, we mostly have to make do with a colourful mixture, but some companies sell them by colour. Stocks are often grown for exhibitions.

For anyone who would like to go into the culture more deeply: there are single and double, summer and winter stocks. The latter are known as 'Bromptons'.

A stock which, according to the enthusiast, should be 'smelled but not seen', is *Matthiola bicornis*. Some seed strewn here and there ensures a delightful fragrance. Night-scented stock is a lavender-coloured cultivar.

Melampodium *Melampodium paludosum*, a new star in the firmament, has suddenly appeared as a pot plant, but it has not yet penetrated into the seed catalogues.

In proportion to the large bright green leaves, the small zinnia-like flowers stand out like cheerful stars. 'Medaillon' grows to 50 cm in height, 'Discovery' to 30 cm. This perennial cultivated as an annual also does well in pots.

Mentzelia 'New' according to the catalogues, but in an old catalogue we find the *Bartonia aurea*, which is exactly the same as *Mentzelia lindleyi*.

Melampodium paludo-sum 'Medaillon', a nice compact plant for pot or bed.

Left: Stocks, Matthiola, grow them for their fragrance.

103

The large, yellow, scented blooms look like papavers and only open in sunny weather.

The 40-60 cm high bushy plants bloom again if they are cut back after flowering and given extra water and food.

Mentzelia lindleyi

Mina   *Mina lobata* is a close relative of *Ipomoea*. In a sheltered place this climber can easily reach a height of 6 m and has amazing tubular flowers, which are first flame-coloured, then orange, after that yellow and eventually cream-coloured.

And all these colours are on one stem. It is a sturdy climber with nice leaves.

The climber Mina lobata *has surprisingly coloured flowers.*

Mirabilis   *Mirabilis jalapa* is a plant without cultivars. A plant which can have pink, red, yellow and white flowers on one plant and these can even be streaked too, really is a wonder.

The flowers of this 'four o'clock plant' don't open until tea time, and are deliciously perfumed to attract moths.

This 'four o'clock' plant which forms bushes, 60-90 cm high, is long-flowering and can stand in a large pot.

The tubers can be kept, like dahlias, but the plants are usually sown again each year.

Right: the blooms of the 'four o'clock', Mirabilis jalapa, *do not open until tea-time.*

Molucella *Molucella laevi* has nothing to do with Ireland, but is still called 'Bells of Ireland'. The bells are the bell-shaped calyxes which are situated in wreaths around the stems. The pinkish flowers are inconspicuous. The plant is grown for its calyx.

The flower stems, which can grow to a height of one metre, are beautiful in bouquets, either fresh or dried. Sow this plant in mid-May where it is to flower.

White forget-me-nots, Myosotis, *are not only beautiful in the garden.*

Myosotis Forget-me-nots, *Myosotis sylvatica*, are usually grown as biennials. Sow in July, then they will bloom in early spring – just when we need these shy little plants, because forget-me-nots are splendid as a background for tulips. Think of a bed of blue forget-me-nots, where white lily-flowered tulips float above them like butterflies, or green tulips with pink forget-me-nots. Do not expect them to bloom throughout the summer.

Once they have reached their peak it is better to replace them with other summer flowers. The higher cultivars are pretty flowers to pick. 'Blue Giant' reaches 40 cm, 'Blue Basket' 30 cm and 'Blue Ball' 15 cm. The pink 'Carmine King' is a little taller than 'Victoria Rose'. The white 'Snow Queen' is taller than 'Victoria Alba'.

Right: Bells of Ireland, Molucella laevis, *owe their decorative value to their bell-shaped calyxes.*

Nemesia The nemesias used to be available by colour. Later there were only variegated mixtures and now we are back to separate colours again.

There are even bicoloured specimens, the blue with white 'KLM' and the red with white 'National Ensign' ('Mello Red & White', 'Danish Flag'). Nemesias combine very well in pots and containers: in a red container *Nemesia strumosa* 'Fire King', in a blue one *Nemesia versicolor* 'Blue Bird'.

In certain places in the garden, mixtures also look very cheerful. 'Carnival' has warm colours and 'Pastel Shades' ('Tapestry') has sweet, soft colours. *Nemesia antirrhinifolia* is not a hardy nemesia but can be kept and propagated by cuttings. This lilac-coloured nemesia looks very much like *Diascia*.

Nemophila *Nemophila menziesii* with its sky-blue flowers with white hearts, is justly called 'Baby Blue Eyes'. This plant, which grows no taller than 30 cm, is also in white with black spots: 'Snowstorm' and 'Atomaria', and in almost-black with a white edge: 'Pennie Black', 'Discoidalis' and 'Pearl Black'.

The other species often cultivated, *Nemophila maculata,* can be recognised by the purple spot on the edge of every petal, whence the name '5spot'.

Nicandra Apple of Peru, *Nicandra physalodes,* from South-America is sometimes found in the wild. Do not plant this member of the potato family if there are small children around.

Nemesia 'Sutton Blue Gem'with small light-blue flowers.

They are not likely to eat the plant, but they might eat the berries hidden in the 'lantern'. The flowers of this sturdy, strongly branched plant are 'Black Pod' deep-blue, 'Alba' white and then there are also the blue flowers of the species and the larger ones of 'Large Flowered'. They are easy and vigorous plants. The lanterns dry well.

Nicotiana Although the product of this plant, which goes up in smoke, is so much criticised, the species and varieties for the garden are much loved. The 'real' tobacco plant, *Nicotiana tabacum* 'Purpureum', is quite a handsome, fairly hefty plant (1.5 m), with large leaves and clusters of red flowers. The most impressive tobacco plant *Nicotiana sylvestris* is even taller. It can reach a couple of metres and has very large leaves (up to 60 cm) and big clusters of large, pendulous, white flowers, which begin to spread their fragrance towards the evening. Good for in the border, but quite a different story is *Nicotiana langsdorfii*. The greenish-yellow flowers hang from slightly arched stems. There are also very many cultivars of *N. alata* and *N. x sanderae*. It is not always clear to which group these belong. 'Lime Green', for example, as a cultivar of *N. alata* is taller and greener than the more compact cultivars of *N. x sanderae*. The blooms of the Domino-series point more upwards and the plants of the Starship-series are more compact and are suitable for in a pot. 'Havana Lime Green', 'Havana Lime Rose' and 'Havana Appleblossom' are strong 40 cm

The flowers of the tobacco plant from the Domino-series seem to be looking at you. Here, Nicotiana *'Domino Salmon'.*

The shorter Nicotiana *'Prelude Pink' lends colour to beds.*

high plants which bloom profusely. The latter is white with pink. These modern cultivars, however, do not have the fragrance of the 'Grandiflora', whose pendulous white flowers are irresistibly fragrant in the evenings.

Nierembergia *Nierembergia hippomanica* is really a perennial, but is cultivated as an annual. The cultivar 'Purple Robe' grows to 20 cm and is covered until autumn with violet-purple bells with a golden-yellow eye. Gold medal winner 'Mont Blanc' is a lobelia-like plant, bearing white flowers with a yellow eye and highly recommended for hanging baskets in full sun.

If you have enough time and energy for deadheading, you will be rewarded by even more abundant flowers.

Is it an Osteospermum *'Sunny Lady' or could it be a* Dimorphoteca ?

Nigella Gertrude Jekyll was extremely fond of love-in-the-mist and used them in many of her borders. Not surprising therefore that a number of hybrids have been named after her. There are blue, pink and white 'Miss Jekylls', which are still sown a lot. They are semi-double and grow on long strong stems. This makes them suitable as cut flowers in fresh bouquets, while the seed-box is used with dried flowers. A nice light-blue is 'Cambridge Blue' and 'Mulberry Rose' is a pretty pink. Something quite different is *Nigella hispanica* with its larger blue-purple blooms with dark-red stamens and beautiful seed-boxes. *Nigella ori-*

Nierembergia hippomanica *'Mont Blanc', a lobelia-like plant that feels very much at home in a hanging basket.*

entalis 'Transformer' has very extraordinary seed-boxes which, when they are ripe, you can turn into a flower. 'Blue Midget' and 'Dwarf Moody Blue' are low, squat bushes adorned with blue flowers.

Nolana *Nolana paradoxa* is a 15-25 cm high creeper, with blue flowers and a white-edged yellow centre. Cultivars are the blue 'Blue Bird' and the white 'Snowbird'. *Nolana humifusa* is even shorter and has smaller flowers. 'Shooting Star' has lavender-coloured flowers with a dark-purple tinge.

Omphalodes Venus's navelwort. If sown in autumn, this beautiful little plant already blooms in May. Sown in spring, it blooms later. *Omphalodes linifolia* resembles white forget-me-nots and has grey foliage. An ideal plant which seeds itself.

Onopordum *Onopordum acanthium,* the Scotch thistle, begins the first year as a modest silver-grey rosette, but really takes off in the second year and easily reaches three metres.
In addition to this Scotch thistle, *Onopordum arabicum* is grown. The plant looks gorgeous against a dark background, but takes up a lot of room and seeds itself freely.

Nolana humifusa *'Shooting Star', lovely for ground cover or in a pot.*

The Scotch thistle, Onopordum, *a very decorative biennial.*

Next page: a discovery, this Papaver commutatum *'Ladybird'. Combined here with red* Atriplex.

111

Osteospermum *Osteospermum* or *Dimorphoteca*, who knows? To see the real difference, take a look at the *Dimorphoteca*. Quite a bit of messing about goes on with these cuttings and there are very many cultivars on the market. The oddest is 'Whirligig' – the name speaks for itself. The long, narrow ray flowers of this cultivar are rolled up, except at the top. In this way, every ray flower has a round top. There is now a whole 'Whirl-series' in all sorts of colours. This cheerful South-African flower is frequently used in pots.

Osteospermum 'Pink Whirl' has unusual, partly curled petals, which create a 'whirling' effect.

Papaver Annual poppies are *Papaver commutatum, P. rhoeas* and *P. somniferum*. Biennials are the Iceland poppies Papaver nudicaule and *Papaver rupifragum*. The loveliest *P. commutatum* is the 'Ladybird', beautifully red with a big black spot at the foot of each petal. The craziest is the 'Danish flag' or 'Danabrog'. This poppy is red and white. The most well-known cultivars of the wild poppy, *Papaver rhoeas*, are the 'Shirley poppies' from the Rev. Wilkes, who lived in Shirley. This single mixture is also available in double and has also been re-selected, which means that the best have been picked out. 'Fiery Wings' is a mix with gorgeous mother-of-pearl colours. The opium poppy, *Papaver somniferum*, has grey-green foliage and mauve blooms which later form lovely round seed-capsules with stigmas. 'Maxi' has blue flowers. 'Giganteum' has the largest seed-capsules. 'Hen and Chicken' has the strangest, 'Peaniflorum' mixture has the fullest double blooms. The latter is also available by colour. *Papaver rupifragum* develops orange-red flowers the second year, which go well with dark foliage plants.

Papaver nudicaule, the well-known Iceland poppy, is most beautiful in a mixture ('Wonderland Mixed' and 'Aurora Borealis'); the white, yellow, pink, red and orange flowers complement each other well. A pastel-coloured mix is 'Primadonna Pastel'. For colour borders they are available by colour.

There are hanging pelargoniums which you can sow, but these are from cuttings.

Pelargonium

Pelargoniums or geraniums, just like fuchsias, do not really belong in this book. But, as with fuchsias, there are also varieties of pelargonium that you can sow. This was already possible in the 70's for standing (zonal) pelargoniums and since recently it is also possible for hanging pelargoniums. For the real enthusiast, F1-hybrids are on sale in various colours. 'Summer Shower' is a hanging pelargonium which, in spite of its silver medal, still does not match up to the pelargonium from cuttings.

Penstemon

Penstemons are actually perennials, which, because they are only half-hardy, are grown as annuals. They can be grown by seed or by taking cuttings. The seed is often sold as a mixture.

'Tall Bicolor Sensation Mixed' are tall plants with clusters of large bi-coloured flowers. The 'Hyacinth Flowered Mixed' has flowers around

The Iceland poppy, Papaver nudicaule *'Illumination'.*

the stem like hyacinths. These striking blooms flower until late autumn and you can even pick them. For those who find these a bit too colourful, a solution would be 'Sour Grapes'. If you see this *Penstemon* you are lost. The flowers are a mixture of white, soft green and lavender-coloured.

Perilla   *Perilla* used to be a much-loved plant for colourful mosaic beds. Dark-leaved cultivars were used for this; preferably the cultivars with dark, curly leaves.
This foliage plant, which was out of fashion for a while, is making a cautious comeback.
Just like the red-leaved orache and Swiss chard, this plant is lovely with brightly coloured annuals, such as African marigolds, in a red border or next to grey foliage plants. It is not easy to get hold of seed.

Petunia   Petunias are available in so many species, sizes and colours that there is little point in giving names. It is important to know that these plants love sun and often look rather pitiful in cool, rainy weather.
The smaller-flowered multifloras do better in this weather than the large-flowered grandifloras, not to mention the double petunias. These should really be grown in the greenhouse.

Perilla nankinensis 'Atropurpurea Laciniata', almost black, between the grey Senecio and the blue Felicia.

Phacelia campanularia *has gentian-blue bells.*

New among the petunias are the surfinias, which up to now have been propagated by cuttings and not by sowing. These are trailing petunias which, apart from in hanging baskets, are also used as ground cover. The shoots can reach half a metre long.

Phacelia *Phacelia tanacetifolia*, the well-known green fertilizer, can of course also be used in the garden. The beautiful purple-blue flowers, which are also good for picking, must be sown where they are to flower. *Phacelia campanularia* is only half as big as the green fertilizer (25 cm) and has gentian-blue bells, which are white at the bottom and on the outside. The bells of *Phacelia parryi* 'Royal Admiral' are completely blue. *Phacelia congesta* has tiny lavender-blue flowers. *Phacelia viscida* is dark blue with a white centre, *Phacelia purshii* is light blue with white.

Phaseolus You can't find this plant in a seed catalogue for summer flowers? That's right, take a look among the vegetable seeds. The *Phaseolus* can be found among the runner beans. It would be a pity to banish this climbing vegetable to the kitchen garden. The cultivars with orange, orange-red with white or pink, sweet pea-like flowers are pretty enough to grow up a tripod in the border, or climb along a fence. 'Sunset' is pink. 'Red Knight' and 'Scarlet Runner' are orange and 'Painted Lady', a very old cultivar has orange and white flowers.

Phaseolus coccineus *'Painted Lady', a lovely name for an unusual runner bean, with orange and white flowers.*

Next page: Petunia *'Mirage Lavender'.*

117

The beans taste delicious by the way. Thompson & Morgan has *Pha-seolus caracalla* which, according to the *Index* should be called *Vigna caracalla*. This 6 m climber has unusual purple with yellow flowers, which look like snail shells.

Phlox drummondii 'Phlox of Sheep' in harmonious pastel shades.

Phlox The annual *Phlox drummondii* is usually found as a variegated mixture. The 'Twinkle'-mixture with the star-shaped bicoloured flowers is the dread of every 'by colour' gardener. The new 'Phlox of Sheep'-mixture will suit him better. These light pastel shades harmonise so well with each other that together they form a soft pastel sea which combines well with other flowers. There is even double phlox, such as apple-blossom coloured 'Chanal'. The Beauty-series has beautiful single-coloured blooms.

Plectranthus *Plectranthus coleoides* 'Marginatus' and *Plectranthus madagasca-riensis* 'Variegated Mintleaf', which are actually indoor plants, have really come into their own in pots, containers and hanging baskets. They also function happily as ground covering plants. In shade or semi-shade they will make beautiful long shoots. By taking cuttings of these at the end of the summer and keeping them frost-free during the winter, you can have plants again for next year. The plants themselves can spend the winter indoors, but preferably not in the living room, because it is too hot there.

120

Polygonum   *Polygonum orientale* is, according to an old gardening book, a luxury version of a weed. But if this 1.5 m tall plant, with beautiful pinkish-red flower spikes, is mixed with other annuals and perennials, you don't notice this. The name alone, 'kiss-me-over-the-garden-gate' is enough to make you sow it.

The much smaller *Polygonum capitatum* is a perennial, grown as an annual because it is not hardy. It is a fantastic ground covering plant, which hardly reaches 10 cm and is also good in hanging baskets and pots. The leaves are brownish-green and the flowers, which are inside little balls, are pink.

'Victory Carpet' is coral pink, 'Pink Pinheads' light pink and 'Pink Bubbles' old rose. This very charming, sturdy plant can be propagated by cuttings, just like *P. orientale.*

Petunia, verbena and Polygonum capitatum, tastefully arranged.

Portulaca   Rose moss, *Portulaca grandiflora,* only likes a very sunny position and light ground. A bad summer is a disaster. These cheerfully coloured plants with fleshy leaves are usually available in red, yellow, white, pink and purple shades. Thompson & Morgan has a bizarre cultivar, which is bicoloured, lilac with white stripes and spots: 'Sundial Peppermint'.

Only the sunniest spot is suitable for this rose moss, Portulaca grandiflora.

Psylliostachys   Nobody knows what a *Psylliostachys* is, but it can perhaps be guessed through the generic name *suworowii.* This statice was first called

Limonium suworowii. The erect, pink spikes, which look a bit like astilbe, are very suitable for drying.

The brown-leaved castor-oil-plant Ricinus communis *'Carmencita' is an imposing sight.*

Reseda *Reseda odorata* is related to the wild *Reseda lutea* and the weld, *Reseda luteola.* The flowers are inconspicuous, but the scent is heavenly. 'Machet' is 45 cm high, 'Red Monarch', the best red, 25 cm and 'Fragrant Beauty' 35 cm. Bees love them. The plants can be cultivated in pots and can be used in bouquets. Sow this plant at the end of March indoors or in mid-April where it is to bloom. *Reseda alba* has white flower spikes and reaches 60 cm.

Left: Reseda luteola, *weld, still grows in the wild.*

Ricinus The castor-oil-plant, *Ricinus communis,* used to be placed in the middle of round spherical beds, surrounded by a pattern of colourful annuals. The plant stuck out like a giant above the dwarfs. It is impressive to see how big the castor-oil-plant can become in a single season. If they get enough water and food, this can be 2 m. Castor-oil-plants are used as solitaire between sizeable perennials or planted in a large pot. The brown-leaved cultivars 'Impala', 'Carmencita' and 'Gibsonii' are the most beautiful. Soak the seeds before sowing. Be careful; they are poisonous!

Rudbeckia The special thing about the sunny annual rudbeckias, *Rudbeckia hirta,* is that they flower late. When other annuals, exhausted by flowering, have given up the ghost, the rudbeckias start to bloom and keep this up until the first frosts. The higher cultivars are good cut flowers. 'Goldilocks' is a double or semi-double mixture, growing to 60 cm. 'My Joy' is yellow with a dark-brown centre, just as you imagine a real rudbeckia to be. Unusual is 'Irish Eyes' ('Green Eyes'), because the centre is green. The 'Gloriosa Daisies' (1.2 m) are tall and have exceptionally large blooms. 'Rustic Dwarfs Mixed' is somewhat shorter. (60 cm).

Salpiglossis   *Salpiglossis sinuata*, painted tongue, was almost forgotten. This relation of the petunia used to be found in nearly every garden and was even a cut flower. It does not like bad weather and prefers a sheltered place. The *Salpiglossis* does well in a pot on the veranda. The Bolero-mixture is 50 cm high and has brilliant orange, red, yellow and pink flowers. The Casino-mixture is not so tall. 'Kew Blue' has beautiful violet-blue flowers.

Salvia coccinea *'Lady in Red', strikingly red, but modest enough for the border.*

Salvia   There are so many different salvias that there is something for everyone. The common red *Salvia splendens* has somewhat less bright purple sisters 'Laser Purple' and 'Phoenix Purple'. They are also in white, salmon and lavender.
Salvia patens 'Cambridge Blue' is light blue and on sale as a plant. 'Oxford Blue' is dark blue and can be sown. Salvias can overwinter if kept frost-free. *Salvia horminum*, now *S. viridis*, is a good cut flower,

Rudbeckias bloom until late autumn.

Left: Salvia viridis
'Pink Sunday' is
a good cut flower
thanks to its
striking bracts.

which fits into the border excellently – thanks to the striking blue, pink or white bracts.

Salvia farinacea is a beautiful, somewhat lavender-like plant, which is perfect in perennial borders. The blue 'Blue Bedder' is very tall. 'Victoria Blue' and 'Renaissance' are much shorter. *Salvia coccinea* is a very unusual plant, up to 1 metre high and with wreaths of fiery-red blooms. The cultivar 'Lady in Red', a gold medal winner, is only half as high. Both plants are magnificent in a red border. Two special biennials are *Salvia argentea* and *Salvia sclarea*. The first is grown for its beautiful silver leaves – the flower stems are usually removed. The second, clary, a striking plant, which in the second year makes flower stems 1 metre long, with lilac-coloured flowers and striking white to pink bracts.

Sanvitalia procumbens, *a charming, abundantly flowering creeper, does well in hanging baskets.*

Sanvitalia   A friendly plant, with little yellow flowers and a clear dark centre. *Sanvitalia procumbens* can be used as ground cover and in pots and hanging baskets, where this creeper drapes itself elegantly over the edge. 'Golden Carpet' has golden-yellow flowers and 'Mandarin Orange' speaks for itself.

Scabiosa   Annual scabiosas, *Scabiosa atropurpurea*, are usually sold as a mixture. The colours go well together in the garden and in a vase. 'Imperial Mixture' has large blooms on long stems. 'Dwarf Double Mixed'

and 'Double Mixed' are taller and have short, double flowers. 'Blue Cockade' is lavender-blue.

You can sow them as early as August. If the seedlings overwinter in a cold frame, they can be planted out in April. But you can also sow indoors in March/April. If you want to sow in one colour, sow a mixture one year and take seed from the best colour. *Scabiosa stellata* 'Drumstick' ('Paper Moon') has quaint round seed-capsules, which you can dry.

The poor man's orchid, Schizanthus pinnatus, *must have a very sheltered place. In a greenhouse these 'Giant Hybrids' bloom profusely.*

Scaevola   *Scaevola aemula* is only propagated through cuttings. A few years ago no one had heard of this plant, but you see it everywhere now. It is a very strong plant and excellent for pots and hanging baskets. 'Blue Fan' is purple-blue, 'Mauve Cluster' is bluer and the flowers are smaller.

Cuttings root quite easily and the plants branch out better if you pinch out the top of the young plants.

Schizanthus   This is a plant which, in the old days, brought credit to the gardener. The plants were grown in pots and exhibited in the greenhouse or the conservatory or brought into the house for decoration. They are still grown for exhibitions and we try very hard to show the 'poor man's orchid', *Schizanthus pinnatus*, at its best.

Scaevola aemula *is propagated through cuttings.*

In the garden these plants can only be put in shady and sheltered spots. The 'Disco'-mix does not grow to more than 40 cm and 'Star Parade' and 'Sweet Lips' are even shorter. They are contented to be in a pot with a roof over their heads.

Senecio   *Senecio cineraria* is not a flowering plant, it is a foliage plant. As an annual it never blooms. 'Silverdust', the most well-known, has very finely divided leaves. The leaves of 'Cirrus' are less incised and it looks more robust. These foliage plants look good in planters. Sow early for good-sized plants.

Silene   *Silene coeli-rosa*, the campion, is often listed in the catalogue as *Viscaria coeli-rosa* or *Lychnis coeli-rosa*.
They are exceptionally friendly plants; the higher cultivars of these can stand in the border and the shorter ones in pots. There are mixtures in bright colours, pink, red, white: 'Brilliant Mixed' and in softer colours: 'Treasure Island Mixed'. By colour they are available in blue, pink and white. Sow them where they are to bloom, because they do not like being transplanted.

Silybum   The milk thistle, *Silybum marianum*, is grown for its leaves. They are impressive to look at – dark green with white markings. The plant is a

Senecio cineraria 'Silverdust', *a foliage plant often cultivated in combination with summer flowers.*

biennial, it makes a rosette the first year and blooms the second year. But the flowers are not what we want. If we don't want milk thistles everywhere, the flowers need to be cut out before they make seed. A hedge of milk thistles creates an very unusual effect. The neighbour's cat will not like it.

The smaller flowered African marigolds, Tagetes tenuifolia, *are also good for picking.*

Sutera   *Sutera cordata,* propagated by cuttings, came on to the market some years ago as *Bacopa.* This ground creeper is very well suited for pots and hanging baskets.

It only needs a few plants to drape themselves around the pot like a skirt and bloom from the last frost to the first frost. They are almost more at home in the shade than in the sun and even manage to grow and flower in places where the sun never comes. The flowers are tiny, white and inconspicuous. A lovely, strong plant.

Tagetes   No front garden without the well-known African marigold, preferably with lots of dark earth between them. These plants deserve better – some of them anyway, not those with the big blooms on cramped little plants. That size bloom (of the Erecta-group) belongs on long stems, so that you can pick them and enjoy the characteristic African marigold smell.

Try putting a group of the Patula-group together in a pot, or put them among the carrots in the vegetable garden to drive away the eelworms.

The African marigold with the smallest flower, *Tagetes tenuifolia*, can go in the garden.

But plant them by colour: lemon-yellow with 'Lemon Gem' or brown-red with 'Paprika'. At least then you can combine them with other plants. 'Starfire', a mixture of small flowered tuft-formers, fits inside a box hedge.

The double feverfew, Tanacetum parthenium *'Butterball', combined with marigolds.*

Tanacetum

Feverfew is known nowadays as *Tanacetum parthenium* and no longer as *Chrysanthemum* or *Matriarca*. The friendly, camomile-like flowers seed themselves freely.

The tall specimens are excellent cut flowers; the single 'Roya' and the double 'Ball's Ultra Double' can reach 80-90 cm. 'Goldball' and 'Butterball' are not so tall (30 cm). The high cultivars are not only good cut flowers but also fit into the border excellently. The shorter strains look good in pots.

Thunbergia

Black-eyed-Susan, *Thunbergia alata,* is a modest climber with lovely orange, yellow or white flowers. Susan's various coloured eyes are usually in a packet as a mixture. She likes a sheltered position and preferably good weather.

Thunbergia fragrans 'Angel Wings' is rather more sensitive, but is worth trying, even if in the conservatory. This plant has fragrant white flowers.

Next page: an extremely beautiful nasturtium is 'Strawberries and Cream'.

Black-eyed-Susan, Thunbergia alata, *a climber for the conservatory or outside in a sheltered position.*

Tithonia The Mexican sunflower, *Tithonia rotundifolia,* a fairly unknown, strapping plant, which can reach 1.5 m and can combine excellently with sunflowers.

'Torch' has orange blooms and its way of growing is nicer than that of 'Goldfinger'. Like sunflowers, the plants need some support when they get very tall. The plants, which have large, heart-shaped leaves and blooms like big zinnias, deserve to be sown more. Indoor sowing is best, by the way.

Tropaeolum Everyone should have nasturtiums, *Tropaeolum majus,* in the garden, even if only to pick the flowers. The bunches of lovely colours are surrounded by wreaths of beautiful round leaves. Don't be afraid that they will run wild; there are enough non-climbing strains. The Whirlybird Hybrids are an unusual series. The unspurred flowers (you don't see it unless you know) stick out above the leaves and look at you. Good examples are 'Cherry Rose' and 'Mahogany'. 'Alaska' has unusual, white marbled foliage which harmonises beautifully with the flowers.

'Empress of India', with dark-red blooms, is still a bestseller. There are some beautifully coloured strains in the Tip Top-series. 'Peach Melba' has a wonderful colour and 'Strawberries and Cream' looks good enough to eat. If you still prefer climbing nasturtiums, there are the 'Gleam Hybrids'. Non-climbing nasturtiums do well in a pot.

The Whirlybird Hybrids of the nasturtiums, like this 'Mahogany' have unspurred flowers which protrude above the leaves.

'Hermine Grashoff' is a very special double variety which, unfortunately, cannot be sown, but must be propagated by cuttings. *Tropaeolum peregrinum*, the canary creeper, is a friendly climber with small yellow flowers.

South African daisies, Ursinia anethoides, *keep their flowers open even when the sun is not shining.*

Ursinia   These South-African daisies keep their flowers open when the sun is not shining.
Ursinia anethoides has lovely orange flowers with a dark circle and a dark centre. It looks good in pots.

Venidium   This South-African Monarch of the Veldt, *Venidium fastuosum*, is orange with a black circle and a black centre. The white 'Zulu Prince' has a large black centre with an orange edge around it. It is a good cut flower, which in bad weather closes on the plant, but once cut, it quickly opens again.

Venidium fastuosum *'Zulu Prince' is an unusually coloured flower which, used with discretion, does not look at all bad in the border.*

Verbascum   *Verbascum blattaria*, mullein, is a magnificent plant, reaching 1.5 m. *Verbascum blattaria* 'Album' (f. *albiflorum* or 'Albiflorum') is an excellent border plant with white, slightly pink shaded flowers with woolly stamens.
Verbascum densiflorum, *Verbascum phlomoides* and *Verbascum thapsus* are all three biennials.
The *Verbascum phlomoides* is the most beautiful to use solitaire.

133

Verbascum phoeniceum is sold as a variegated mixture. The decorative pink, red, purple and white flower spikes reach a height of 1 m. *Verbascum olympicum* has large flowers and can reach 2-3 m in height.

Verbena rigida *'Lilacina' is exceptionally beautiful for combining.*

Verbena   There are many different verbenas: for the garden, in hanging baskets, tall and short verbenas, with or without an eye and all of those in countless colours. Verbena seed must be sown indoors with heat and does not always germinate easily. Many can also be propagated easily from cuttings. Among the verbena-hybrids there is an unusual mixture 'Peaches and Cream' in all shades of apricot, cream, soft orange and yellow.

'Romance Lavender' has lavender-blue flowers. *Verbena rigida* 'Lilacina' is a lovely, fairly tall blue verbena. The dark purple *Verbena speciosa* 'Imagination' does well, both in hanging baskets and as ground cover.

Verbena bonariensis is actually a perennial, but is often grown as an annual. This tall (1.5 m), elegant plant fits excellently into a perennial border and seeds itself.

Viola   It is very pleasant in spring to put pansies in pots and to combine them with spring bulbs such as tulips. If it were left to the growers we would plant pansies the whole year round. The dividing line between the biennial and perennial pansies was never very clear and is now fading away even more because there are cross-matches between *Viola x wittrockiana* with *Viola cornuta*. The result of this cross-matching is charming small-flowered pansies, which should really last longer but are considered as annuals, such as 'Baby Lucia' and 'Baby Franjo'.

Viola tricolor, the three-coloured pansy, has also played a role in all the cross-matches. One pansy of which, as with so many others, the origin cannot be traced, is 'Velour Blue', a lovely pansy with small flowers. *Viola tricolor* 'Nigra' is a small black pansy. 'Super Chalon Giants Mixed' is a mixture of pansies from Thompson & Morgan, with a frill edge.

There is no nicer present than a basket of pansies.

Zinnia

Zinnia elegance, comprises giants and dwarfs. The larger 'Californian Giants' and 'Dahlia Flowered', are excellent cut flowers in beautiful harmonising colours. 'Envy' is a lovely green zinnia, 'Purple Prince' is lilac. Zinnias should preferably not be sown too early. The beginning of May is early enough. You can sow zinnias in the garden where they are to flower when the ground has warmed up after the danger of night frosts has passed. The 'Persian Carpet' mixture is only 40 cm high and consists of bicoloured flowers.

Next page:
Viola *'Velour Blue'*
won a gold medal in 1994.

Zinnia elegans
'Persian Carpet', with flowers in the colour of a Persian carpet, reach a height of 40 cm.

Index

Previous page: Verbascum *likes to seed itself and has to be weeded regularly.*

Acknowledgements

Photography:
George M. Otter
Mineke Kurpershoek pages 126 (margin) and 129 (margin)

Photograph locations:
Holland
Castle gardens Arcen
Garden centre Blomhof, IJsselstein
Marijke van Dijk, Heerle
Laura Dingemans, Heerle
Nursery Coen Jansen, Dalfsen
Nursery Van de Kaa, Dieren
Liesbeth Kappelhof, IJsselstein
Koning family, Aalsmeer
Nursery Overhagen, Velp
De Rhulenhof, Ottersum
Nursery Schoonen, Wouw
Herman Simons, Wouw
Chiel Smit, Lopik
Summer Garden, Enkhuizen
Own garden and along the road
Various garden fairs

England and Scotland
More than sixty gardens and along the road

Botanic gardens
Royal Botanic Garden, Edinburgh, Scotland
Botanic garden of the University of Helsinki, Finland
Botanic garden of the University of Uppsala, Sweden

Grateful thanks to Carla and Gerard Buurman of the Nursery Overhagen for their inspiration, good advice and help with the nomenclature.